WOODEN TOYS

Wooden Toys

Anthony Hontoir

The Crowood Press

First published in 1992 by
The Crowood Press Ltd
Ramsbury, Marlborough
Wiltshire SN8 2HR

British Library Cataloguing in Publication Data

A catalogue record for this book is available from the British Library

ISBN 1 85223 449 0

Line-drawings and photographs by Anthony Hontoir.

Typeset by Footnote Graphics, Warminster, Wiltshire
Printed in Great Britain at The Bath Press

CONTENTS

INTRODUCTION

The making of wooden toys is a most enjoyable pastime that does not require considerable woodworking skill or experience, and need not cost a lot of money. One of its most rewarding aspects is the look of pleasure on the face of a small child when the toy is given, and the many hours of fun that follow.

The toys that appear in this book cover a range of ages and interests, and try wherever possible to appeal to boys and girls. The smallest and simplest projects are intended for the very young, and the pencil dice and clock puzzle have features that help the child to learn.

As it is important for children to play outdoors in the open air, there are toys for the garden. A small table and chair set can be used for holding tea-parties, or for entertaining dolls and teddy-bears. The oval rocker can either be treated as a rocking horse or a see-saw. The toboggan will certainly appeal to the more adventurous child, and is designed for sliding down grass-covered slopes, usually at great speed. The horse tricycle is a more sedate toy for toddlers.

Some of the toys have more than one purpose. For instance, the castle toy box is not only an exciting fortress that houses some medieval king, but also a storage box to help keep the bedroom tidy. The doll's chest of drawers will one day be a jewellery box, when the doll has long since been replaced by other interests. And the windmill will keep turning as long as there are coins to be saved.

The toys are presented mainly in order of difficulty and the amount of material that is needed to make them. Certainly you will require a reasonable outlay on tools, including a jig-saw and router, if that is possible. There are also occasions when it is desirable to turn the wood on a lathe, but small lathe attachments can be mounted on the workbench and driven by ordinary electric drills to give surprisingly good results.

The more woodwork you do, the more you will find that you acquire a large supply of off-cuts, which should never be thrown away but carefully stored in a box somewhere in your workshop. This is not merely an excuse to hoard, because even the smallest scrap of wood will often have a use, and besides, hardwood is quite expensive to purchase, and most of us want to get our money's worth.

Toy-making rarely demands complicated joints, and most of the wood joints employed in this book are abutting, dowelled, lapped and housing. So if you have never practised any woodwork in the past, there is no reason why you should not make a success of the toys described on the following pages.

Tools and Materials

It is possible to produce first-class results in woodwork without elaborate facilities. A limited number of tools and a corner of the kitchen table have in the past provided the enthusiast with sufficient basis upon which to apply the skilled pair of hands and an inspired imagination. After all, toy-making does not usually demand the same methods of production as those employed in other areas of woodwork, such as furniture-making or carpentry and joinery. Toys are often small objects with a simplicity in design and construction.

However, it is always preferable to establish a proper workplace of your own and stock it with a good range of tools, for then you will find that even the most straightforward of tasks is made that much easier, and those projects that at first seemed far too complicated will indeed prove to be less difficult than you imagined.

THE WORKPLACE

Most of us are able to find somewhere suitable around the house to set up a small workshop without causing too much inconvenience. For the majority, it will be at the far end of the garage, or inside the garden shed, whereas for the fortunate few, who live in large properties, there is always a spare room somewhere that can be converted into a workplace.

Once you have found your little niche, you will need to make provision for an effective working surface, normally in the form of a sturdy bench. The choice of workbench is important, especially for larger items of woodwork, and it should be equipped with a proper carpenter's vice, a solid top surface, a recessed tool tray and a bench stop.

The workbench can be made all the more versatile by the use of the simple bench-hook for holding awkwardly shaped pieces of wood, and by making provision for a vertical drill stand to be installed at one end, allowing an electric drill to be manipulated with great precision. An assorted range of G-clamps are essential for holding pieces of wood securely to the end of the workbench.

The workplace should also have a good solid floor, plenty of light and a power supply.

HANDTOOLS

When you have found somewhere convenient to work, the next step is to build up a collection of good woodworking tools. For the making of toys, it is not so important to have a large number of tools at your disposal, because many of the cutting out and shaping operations may be carried out successfully with only a few basic handtools. However, it is more than likely that toy-making is only one of several woodworking activities with which the enthusiastic woodworker is engaged, so it is fair to assume that the tools acquired will also be used for other purposes.

No doubt you will already possess a few items – most of us accumulate a variety of tools over the years – but if you do need to add to the collection, make a point of buying well-known brand names that can be relied upon for their high quality and long working life. Cheap tools are invariably a false economy.

Let us consider which tools you should aim to include in your tool cabinet.

The Pencil

Always keep one or two pencils readily to hand, and a pencil sharpener to ensure that they retain a fine point. Do not use a pencil with a hard lead, because this will score the surface of the wood and the marks could prove difficult to remove later at the sandpapering stage. Nor do you want a very soft lead, because this quickly loses its fine point and you end up drawing thick lines. An HB lead is a good compromise.

The Tape Measure

All woodworking depends for its success on accurate measurement, and the rule or tape measure is probably used more than any other single tool. The spring-loaded flexible steel tape measure pulls out from a metal casing, has a lock to hold it in any position, and retracts back into the casing when not in use. The scale is marked on one face in inches and centimetres, with an L-shaped steel lip serving to mark the zero position.

The Pair of Compasses

As there are many occasions when you will need to mark circles accurately on the surface of a piece of wood, you should include a pair of geometrical compasses in the tool cabinet. The best sort are those used as precision drawing instruments, with the pointed pin and the lead held in adjustable sleeves.

The Marking Knife

Although this is normally used when the marking calls for a thin line to be scribed on the surface of the wood, the marking knife may also be employed to cut right through thin pieces of material, such as plywood, in preference to using a saw. The Stanley knife is ideal, because it has a handle that fits easily into the palm of the hand and a guard to fit over the blade when not in use. Spare blades can be bought in packets and are easy to replace.

The Bradawl

This is a marking tool which has a handle shaped rather like that of a screwdriver, and is fitted with a short steel spike which terminates in a sharp point. The purpose of the bradawl is to start off screw holes and help to prevent the wood from splitting.

The Square

When marking out wood in readiness for cutting, it is usual practice to draw a line at right-angles to its length. The square consists of a rectangular wooden handle, edged in brass, which has a steel blade attached to it at 90 degrees with two parallel edges.

The Marking Gauge

This tool, used for scribing a single line along a piece of wood, has a wooden stock in which a hardened steel spur is mounted at one end, and a sliding wooden fence that can be locked in any position. Strictly speaking, the marking gauge is designed to mark lines that run in the same direction as the wood grain. For marking across the grain, a slightly different tool called a cutting gauge is used, which has a sharp steel blade instead of a spur, to cut through the fibres of the wood without tearing or snatching. However, with care the marking gauge can be used for both purposes.

The Mortise Gauge

Similar in appearance to the marking gauge, the mortise gauge differs in that it has two spurs, one of which is adjustable, so that two parallel lines can be marked on the wood. The best types of mortise gauge are equipped with a rounded brass thumbscrew at the opposite end from the spurs, to control the position of the inner moveable spur with great precision. As with the marking gauge, the wooden fence is released and tightened by means of a screw. Most mortise gauges combine two functions by having double spurs on one side of the stock to mark mortises, and a single spur on the opposite side to provide a marking facility.

The Handsaw

This is a general-purpose saw used for doing most preparatory cutting. The teeth are set in an alternating pattern so that as the saw cuts into the wood, it creates a passage known as the kerf that is wider than the thickness of the blade, thus ensuring that it does not bind or jam. This type of saw is designed for cutting at right-angles to the direction of the grain, though, in practice it is often called upon to cut with the grain also.

The Tenon Saw

As its name suggests, the tenon saw is mostly used for cutting tenons and other types of joint. It is shorter than the handsaw, and the top edge of the blade is strengthened with a steel or brass back to give rigidity and ensure a straight cut. As many of the toys described in this book use relatively small sections of wood, the tenon saw is recommended for general cutting in preference to the handsaw.

The Coping Saw

A very useful saw when you need to cut curves. The thin blade is mounted in a metal frame shaped in the form of a U, and held under tension by tightening the handgrip. If the handgrip is slackened off, the blade can be rotated about its axis within the frame to set it at any desired angle. As the blade can be removed from the frame, the coping saw can be used to cut internal holes within the wood by first drilling through the piece with the brace and bit, inserting the free end of the blade, and re-attaching it to the frame before commencing the cut.

The Hacksaw

The hacksaw bears a close resemblance to the coping saw, because the blade is held in a metal frame and can be changed when the teeth wear down. The difference is that the teeth are much finer and the blade cannot be rotated. The hacksaw is mostly used for cutting metal, but it is equally useful for sawing hardwood dowel or similar material, when the fineness of the blade makes for a smooth, light cut.

The Chisel

It is advisable to have a set of chisels covering a range of sizes so that you can select the most suitable width of blade for the job in hand. Typical blade widths are 6mm (¼in), 9mm (⅜in), 13mm (½in), 16mm (⅝in), 19mm, (¾in) 22mm (⅞in), and 25mm (1in), although it is not necessary to include each of these sizes in the set. There are various types of chisel, and each has its own particular characteristics. For instance, the firmer chisel has a strong cutting blade with square edges, and is used for cutting mortises and similar joints; whereas the bevelled chisel, in which the two edges of the blade are sloped, makes the tool ideal for cutting dovetail joints, or any other sort of work where an adjacent edge of wood forms less than 90 degrees. Indeed, the bevelled chisel has a much wider application because the steel from which the blade is forged has such strength that it can be employed for most cutting tasks.

The Smoothing Plane

This is the most frequently used bench plane and, as far as toy-making is concerned, the best choice for planing down sawn edges of wood and preparing chamfers and bevels.

The Spokeshave

The function of the spokeshave is mainly to shape curved surfaces that have already been cut with the coping saw or jig-saw, but that would be impossible to smooth down with the flat smoothing plane. The spokeshave can be put to many other uses, including the preparation of chamfers and bevels in short lengths of wood, and for chamfering the ends of large-diameter dowelling.

The Plough Plane

Also known as the combination plane, this tool consists of a cast iron body to which the blade is attached, together with the handle. Two parallel steel rods protrude sideways from the body of the plane and carry the adjustable cast-iron fence. There is a depth guide that can be raised or lowered to suit the nature of the cut. A range of cutters can be fitted to the plough plane, providing a variety of operations: grooving, filleting, reeding, rebating and preparing edge mouldings.

The Brace Drill

This tool is used for the majority of drilling operations. It consists of a crank forged from steel that is fitted with a rounded wooden or plastic handle at one end and a chuck at the other, for holding a variety of drill bits.

The Hand Drill

A more compact type of drill than the brace, the hand drill does not have a crank, but the motive power is supplied by turning a wheel that is set midway along the frame and geared to two pinions that turn the chuck. The drilling action is firm and positive, but does not provide the same torque, or turning effect, as the brace. The hand drill is ideally suited to light drilling work.

Drill Bits

These provide the drill with its cutting edge. Those used in the brace are square-tanged so that they can be gripped by the chuck, but power drills usually only accept bits that have round shanks. The hand drill, depending on the type of chuck fitted, will take either one or the other.

For drilling very small diameter holes in wood or plywood, the twist drill is best and it has the advantage that it may also be used for boring holes through metal or plastic. Medium sized holes, ranging from 6mm (¼in) to 13mm (½in) in diameter, should be drilled with long spiral-shaped auger bits, particularly for boring a straight hole deep into end-grain, as in the preparing of dowel joints. Larger-diameter holes can be made with the centre bit, which resembles the cutting tip of the auger bit but does not have a long spiral shaft. Finally, for much larger holes, or for the cutting of round discs, there is the multi-blade hole saw set that has a range of blade diameters, each of which may be mounted securely on a circular frame and a mandrel, or central axle, which cuts a pilot hole and thus fixes the position of the round saw blade before it comes into contact with the wood.

The Wooden Mallet

The mallet is used whenever a blow needs to be struck in the course of cutting joints and assembling the work – with the exception of driving in nails. The mallet's large head is usually made from beech, and the handle, which is wedge-shaped to prevent the head from flying off, is often cut from ash. Both materials are very hard and durable.

The Hammer

A light joiner's hammer is useful for knocking in small nails and panel or veneer pins. The head is forged from steel and the handle made from ash.

The File

A tool widely used in metalwork, the file has a more limited role as far as toy-making is concerned. It is used only to erase minor imperfections and leave a smooth, clean edge in areas where tools such as the plane and spokeshave cannot reach. The standard shape for the file is flat on both sides, but there are other types that offer a half-round surface, triangular and circular cross-sections, of which the last example is usually referred to as the 'rat-tail' file. They each have an abrasive surface, made up of many rows of tiny teeth, and vary in the degree of roughness. A very coarse type would be unsuitable for most aspects of woodwork, because even the hardest of woods yield to the backward and forward rubbing action of a finely patterned file. You will notice that one end of the file always comes to a point, known as the tang and, for safety's sake, you should fit a wooden handle to prevent the sharp end digging into your palm.

POWER TOOLS

The Electric Jig-Saw

In its most common form, this is a hand-held power tool in which the saw blade oscillates up and down at very high speed to provide a fast and highly manoeuvrable means of cutting. Some of the more expensive models have a range of speed settings, and a knob may be provided to turn the blade. There are many occasions when the jig-saw is an invaluable tool, especially when cutting around curved lines. However, certain materials such as plywood and chipboard, can wear the blade down very rapidly and reduce the effectiveness of the cut – so the blade must be inspected regularly and replaced once the teeth become dulled.

The Electric Plane

A high-speed tool that performs much the same work as the smoothing plane, except that the physical effort is reduced and the task of planing down the wood made a lot quicker. There is a knob for raising or lowering the sole at the front and thus altering the depth of the cut. The electric plane is particularly useful if you are preparing your own sections of wood from sawn timber.

The Electric Drill

The hand-held electric drill is suitable for many drilling jobs, and some of the more expensive models are provided with variable speed operation. However, where the drill really comes into its own is when it is mounted in a vertical drill stand to facilitate precision drilling, or when it is used to provide the motive power for workbench-mounted lathe accessories, permitting a limited amount of wood-turning.

The Electric Router

This is probably the most specialised tool that the woodworker is likely to buy, with the possible exception of a lathe, and it is well worth setting enough money aside to purchase a good one. There is always an element of mystery about a tool that has a reputation for performing many functions, in this case rebating, edge-moulding, grooving and fluting, to name but a few. In fact, the electric router is simply a motor housed vertically inside the body of the tool, which drives the chuck at very high revolutions. Into the chuck may be fitted a wide range of cutters. Because the cutter turns at such a high speed, it produces a very clean cut regardless of whether the router is moved along in the same direction as the grain or at right-angles to it, making this tool more versatile than the plough plane. The base of the router is circular, so that it can be lined up beside a length of straight-edged batten, acting as its guide and steered at any angle without deviating from a straight path. A detachable fence can be mounted beneath the base to provide the router with its own adjustable guide – or a special plate enables it to cut in a circle – and the spring-loaded plunging action of the body can be pre-set against a scaled depth stop so that the cutter is accurately controlled both laterally and vertically.

The Lathe

This is such a highly specialised piece of equipment that you would not be likely to purchase one unless you were planning to carry out a lot of wood-turning. For occasional turnery, the answer is either to buy a small workbench-mounted lathe, or a lathe accessory powered by an electric drill, or to find a local workshop that is prepared to hire its facility for a reasonable fee. The hand-tools most commonly used when wood-turning are the spindle gouge, the chisel and the parting tool, each of which will require practice in its use before successful results are obtained.

STORAGE AND CARE OF TOOLS

All woodworking tools must be carefully looked after if they are to produce good results, and this means keeping them clean and sharp, and storing them correctly when not in use. The most practical method of storage is the tool cabinet, which can be hung on the wall near your place of work.

From time to time, cutting tools will need to be resharpened if they are to produce consistently first-class work. Handsaws and tenon saws have their blades correctly set and fully sharpened when you buy them – but, inevitably, they wear down after prolonged use. The blunting effect of certain hardwoods only hastens the process. Check the teeth regularly, and, at the first sign of wear, arrange for the blade to be resharpened. You can obtain special sharpening tools to do the job yourself, but the better course of action is to take the saw to your local tool dealer and ask for the teeth to be sharpened and re-set by a specialist.

The blades of the coping saw, hacksaw and jig-saw are detachable, so the task of keeping them sharp is simply a matter of taking off the old blunt saw blade and replacing it with a new one. Jig-saw blades come in a wide range of teeth sizes and pitches.

The sharpening of the blade of a chisel, smoothing plane or spokeshave is carried out on an oilstone, and is probably one of the most basic and routine maintainance tasks that you will have to perform.

CHOICE OF WOOD

One of the points constantly made throughout this book is that the making of small wooden toys gives you the opportunity to use up pieces of off-cut material left over from other projects, for it is reasonable to assume that, if you are sufficiently interested in woodwork to indulge in the making of toys, you probably already spend part of your time building other items for the home. The contents of the waste bin may take years to accumulate, but even the smallest pieces of left-over wood will have a use one day.

If toy-making is a new interest, you will find that most timber merchants are prepared to sell relatively small quantities of wood, and they have waste bins from which you might be able to salvage just the material you want.

As most of the toys in this book are intended to be painted, the choice of wood is not absolutely critical, and you should be able to decide for yourself whether to use one sort or another. In this respect, the colour of the wood is not nearly as important as its texture and grain structure, since these are the characteristics that will affect the way it responds to cutting and shaping.

Most of the woods employed in the various projects are of the hardwood type, because hardwood usually produces a better result. Among the available varieties of hardwood, oak, sapele, utile, beech and ash are used most; whereas from the category defined as softwood, parana pine is an excellent example for producing clean, knot-free surfaces, and the cheaper redwood can be used when the quality of the material is not so important.

Plywood and hardboard are frequently used, in varying thicknesses and these may be purchased from most DIY shops, as indeed can the dowelling and the hardwood strips that are so often needed. For the thinnest sizes of plywood and the smallest diameters of dowelling, the best source of supply is undoubtedly a model shop, which also stocks a useful range of wheels, axles and hub caps.

GLUES AND ADHESIVES

The strength of a good glue lies in its ability to spread in liquid form across the full extent of the joining surfaces, covering a relatively big area. If you could examine the surface of the wood in microscopic detail, you would discover that no matter how smooth it appears to the naked eye or feels to the touch, it is, in fact, totally irregular and full of tiny cavities. The glue, possessing the capacity to flow, searches out these holes or crevices and fills them. As it begins to set, the internal molecular structure of the glue locks into a chain and eventually becomes a single solid mass, often stronger than the wood itself.

The conditions necessary for a successful bond are that the two joining surfaces be clean, dry and free from traces of oil or grease. Once the glue has been applied to both parts of the joint, it is assembled and clamped firmly together for a period of time while the glue sets hard.

Powdered Resin Glue

Although there seems to be an apparently endless list of synthetic substances on the market, our interest is chiefly concentrated on the urea formaldehyde powdered resin type, to which a measured quantity of cold water must be added and stirred in thoroughly, making an active and workable mixture that is ready for use within a matter of a few seconds. An old cup will serve as a suitable mixing vessel and an old spoon as a means of measuring out the powder and the water. To apply the glue, use a small, cheap artist's paintbrush. Temperature does not play a critical role in the use of this glue as it does with Scotch glue, but an ambient temperature of at least 15°C (59°F) is desirable.

Ready-Mixed Liquid Glue

This is another synthetic glue that does not need any preparation whatsoever, but can be applied directly to the workpiece, straight from the tube or bottle. By chemical composition it is known as polyvinyl acetate (PVA).

Epoxy Resin Adhesive

For making a very powerful bond between wood and metal, wood and plastic or plastic and metal, an epoxy resin adhesive is probably the best choice. It is supplied in two tubes: one contains the adhesive, the other the hardening agent. As long as the two substances are kept separate, nothing happens, but when equal amounts are squeezed out and mixed thoroughly together, a catalytic reaction takes place and the adhesive begins to set. Some epoxy resins set within minutes and others take several hours.

SAFETY PRECAUTIONS

Accidents usually happen very quickly and can be avoided by taking care at all times. Tools such as the saw and the chisel should always be kept sharp if they are to be effective in cutting the wood, but this means that they will be devastatingly effective in cutting fingers that happen to get in the way. When you have to hold the workpiece with your free hand, keep it well out of the saw's reach, and behind the blade of the chisel.

Certain types of wood contain substances that can cause blood poisoning, so if you get a splinter under the skin, remove it immediately and bathe the affected area with antiseptic lotion.

Always take adequate precautions when using power tools – such as the wearing of protective goggles to cover your eyes, a face mask to avoid inhaling fine dust particles and ear-muffs to safeguard your hearing from the loud whine of an electric planer, router or jig-saw. Switch off power tools when they are not in use, isolating their plugs from the power supply. Never let wood shavings or sawdust accumulate on the workbench or the surrounding floor, because they are a potential fire risk as well as a menace for slipping on.

When applying glue or varnish to the wood, take care not to get any on your skin. If you do pick up traces on your fingers, wash them off immediately with plenty of soap and water.

CHAPTER ONE

THE PENCIL DICE

A pair of large wooden dice will provide plenty of amusement and, for the older child, can be used to learn to count up to twelve. The dice have a second purpose, for the holes in the number six face are drilled deeper than those on the other five faces, and are meant for storing pencils.

It might seem at first sight that there could hardly be anything simpler than making a pair of dice – just cut out two cubes of wood and make a few holes here and there with the drill. In a way, this is true because there is no jointing to be done – but the preparation of each cube does require a certain amount of precision and skilled manipulation of the spokeshave.

The cubes are identical, so once you have made one, the same method applies thereafter, even if you wish to increase or decrease the size.

The choice of wood is important. It should be a hard, relatively dense wood that will not dent too easily as it is thrown about. But it should also be a wood that works well with handtools, suggesting an even-grained hardwood. The illustrated dice are made from beech.

Start by preparing a length of material to cross-sectional dimensions of 65× 65mm (2½×2½in), noting that it is important for the wood to be exactly square in end-grain. Divide it up into cubes by checking the measurement of the width and thickness, and marking this amount along its length, squaring all around. Cut out each cube with the jig-saw, as the high speed action of this particular tool – fitted with a fine-toothed blade – gives a very smooth cut across the end-grain.

Dice are not really perfectly square-shaped cubes of wood. Usually the corners are rounded off so that they roll more easily. The rounding off must be carried out equally for each corner, other-

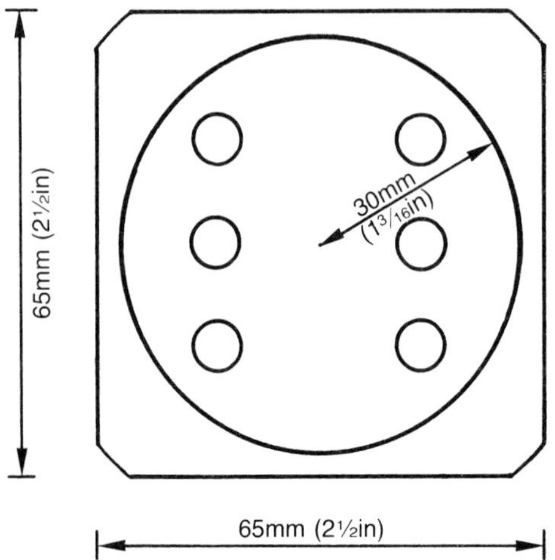

Main dimensions of the dice.

Mark a circle on each of the cube's six faces with a pair of compasses.

wise the element of pure chance will be lost when each die is rolled.

Find the centre of all six faces by drawing a straight line between diagonally opposite corners, the centre of each face being the point at which the two lines intersect.

Now take a pair of geometrical compasses and set them to a radius of 30mm (1³⁄₁₆in), assuming that the cube measures 65×65×65mm (2½×2½×2½in), and draw a circle on all six faces. The circumference will come within 2.5mm (⅛in) of each edge.

Clamp the block in the vice and start trimming away the waste from the corners with the spokeshave, planing off a little at a time, and aiming to maintain a perfectly rounded contour simultaneously between the three adjacent surfaces. This will entail changing the block's position in the vice so that the trimming can be carried out from different directions.

Take care with every cut not to manipulate the spokeshave beyond the marked circles. Finish off by rubbing down the corners firstly with medium-grade sandpaper, and then fine-grade to give the smoothest possible surface.

If you wish to avoid using the hand-held spokeshave and have access to a workbench lathe, and the necessary experience in using it, the corners of the dice can be rounded off by wood-turning. Of course you will still have to prepare the cubes of wood in the same way, and mark out the circle on each of the six faces; and there is one other step in the preparation that is important if the block is to be mounted in the lathe.

The block cannot be placed directly between the headstock and tailstock of the lathe, otherwise two of its faces would be irreparably damaged. An alternative means must be employed to secure the

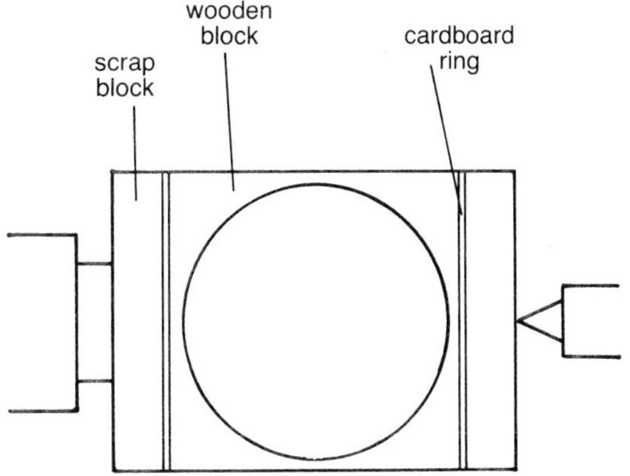

Scrap blocks are attached for lathe-turning, and the assembly mounted between the headstock and tailstock of the lathe.

block between the centres. Small pieces of scrap wood are attached to serve as buffers and thus prevent the headstock and tailstock from making direct contact with the cube.

The scraps can be of any type of wood, but they should be approximately 13mm (½in) in thickness. Taking the geometrical compasses, still set to a radius of 30mm (1³⁄₁₆in), draw two circles on the waste material equal in size to the circles described on the six faces of the cube, and cut these out carefully with either the coping saw or jig-saw.

Similarly, cut out two circles from thin cardboard, also measuring 30mm (1³⁄₁₆) in radius.

Mix a quantity of wood glue and make a sandwich on each of the block's two end-grains, consisting of the thin cardboard glued to the end grain and the circular piece of scrap wood glued on to the card, each of these being mounted exactly inside the circular marking on the wood.

As these scrap blocks are assembled on opposite sides of the cube, they may be clamped together while the glue dries.

The centres of the scrap blocks are clearly indicated by the tiny point made by the pair of compasses in marking out the circle, and these two points are taken as the positions in which to mount the cube in the lathe.

Set the wood turning and round off the corners with the spindle gouge, stopping the lathe frequently to check that you do not remove too much waste. As you approach the marked circles, including the two circles on the end-grain to which the scrap blocks are attached, use less pressure on the spindle gouge, switching to medium-grade sandpaper to complete the rounding off of the corners.

The protruding point of a panel pin ensures that the scrap block can be located absolutely centrally, by aligning with the mark made by the compasses. As the scrap block is placed on the cube, the pin is pushed back.

Take the shaped die out of the lathe and remove the protective waste blocks by simply chiselling down into the cardboard layer. Clean off the cardboard and glue from the two end-grains by a combination of scraping and sandpapering until the wood surfaces are restored.

Mark the one-to-six pattern of dots on the six faces of the dice, referring to the following sequence: number six is uppermost with number one on the bottom face; then, rotating the dice clockwise, the order is four, five, three and two. If in doubt, you will probably have board-

Mount the block between the headstock and tailstock of the lathe, and carefully round off the corners, keeping just within the limits of the marked circles. The two scrap blocks delineate the two end circles.

When the woodturning is complete, remove the scrap blocks by striking down into the cardboard sandwich with the tip of a wide-bladed chisel.

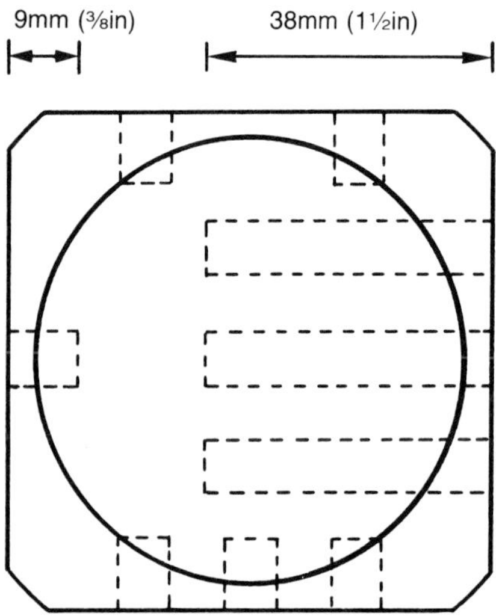

The hole depths in the six-face, relative to the remaining five faces.

Mark out the holes in the six faces, and drill out with a 13mm (½in) centre bit.

games available that normally include a pair of small plastic dice.

Measure out and mark in the positions of the numbers and drill them into the wood using a 13mm (½in)-diameter auger bit or centre bit. For the six face, which will be used to store pencils, drill each hole to a depth of 38mm (1½in); and for the five remaining faces, drill to a depth of 9mm (⅜in).

The dice can either be painted, varnished or polished, a polish possibly providing the best type of finish.

Cutting List

Wooden block: two of 65×65×65mm (2½×2½×2½in)

CHAPTER TWO

THE TABLE-TOP SKITTLES

The game of table skittles, when it is played on a small square board, is a simple variation of the popular pastime played in a skittle alley, in which nine or ten pins are set up at one end and bowled over with a large wooden ball. In

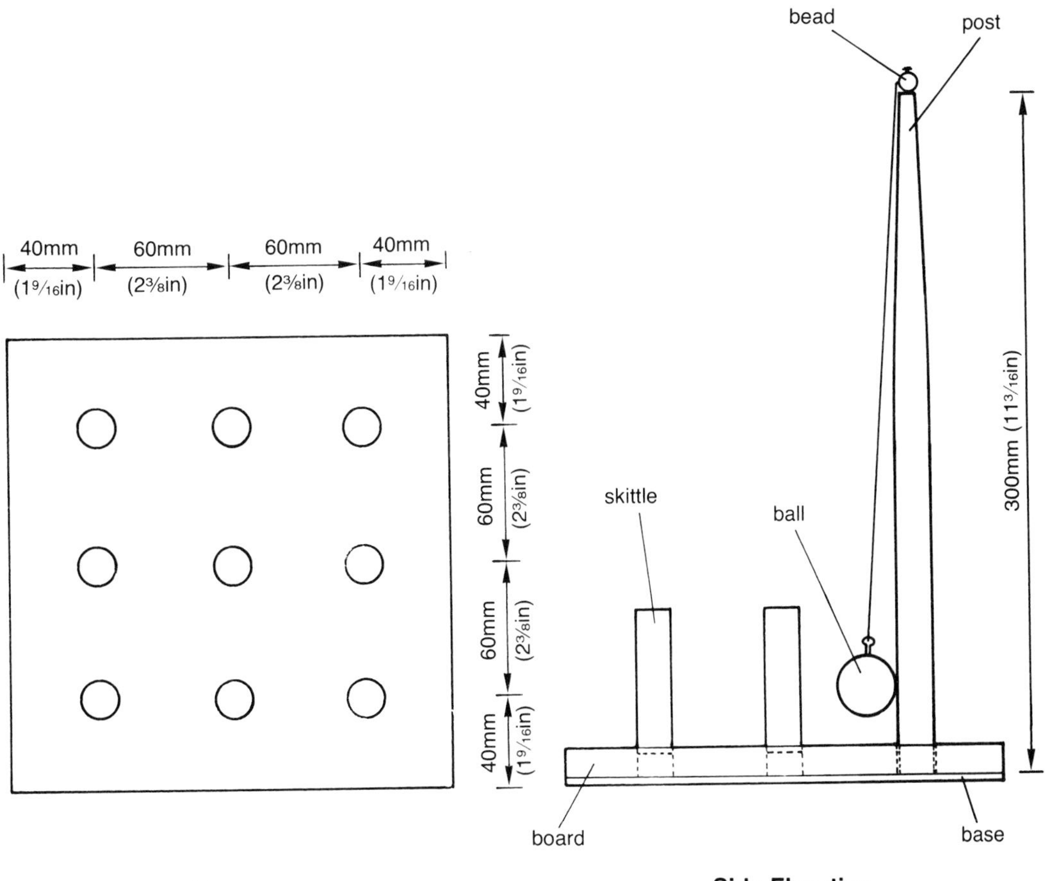

Main dimensions of board and base assembly.

this version, adapted to suit a young child, the skittles, eight in number, are placed in shallow holes arranged in a square board, and the ball is swung on the end of a long string attached to the top of a supporting pole placed at one corner of the board.

The material requirements are very basic, and the method of construction is simple and straightforward. The board is made from plywood and hardboard bonded together, the skittles and the post are lengths of dowelling and the ball is a wooden bead that can be obtained from any craft shop.

Start by marking out two identical squares, each measuring 200×200mm ($7\frac{7}{8}$x$7\frac{7}{8}$in), one on a piece of 13mm ($\frac{1}{2}$in)-thick birch-faced plywood and the other on a sheet of 4mm ($\frac{3}{16}$in) hardboard. Cut them out with the jig-saw, taking care to keep the edges perfectly straight.

Measure and mark out a pattern of nine holes on the upper surface of the plywood – actually, at this early stage, there is no difference in appearance between what you might call the upper and lower surface, except that it is usual to choose for the visible side the one that seems that little bit better. The holes are arranged regularly in three rows of three. The four holes at the corners are set 40mm ($1\frac{9}{16}$in) in from each adjacent edge, and all the other holes are then placed equi-distantly.

Take a 16mm ($\frac{5}{8}$in)-diameter centre bit, mount it in the handbrace and drill right through the plywood in the nine marked positions. Do not attempt to drill through in one go, otherwise the plywood will splinter badly on the opposite

Cut the board to size with the jig-saw.

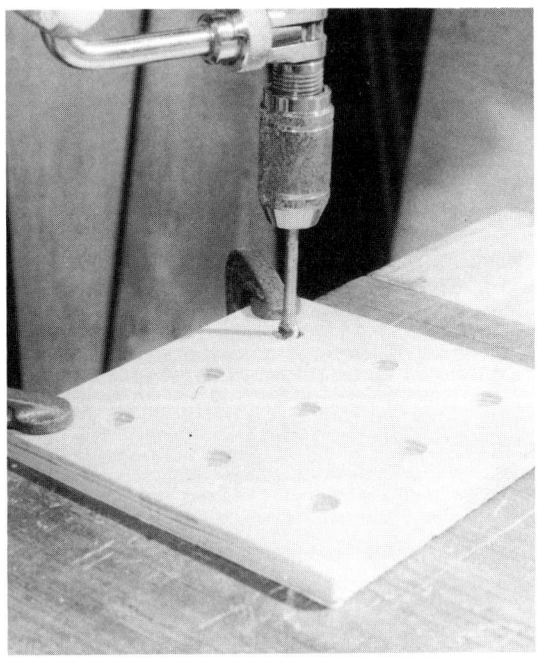

Measure and mark the nine holes in the board, and drill them out with a 16mm (⅝in) centre bit.

side as the bit emerges. Instead, stop turning the handbrace as soon as the point of the drill-bit breaks through, then turn the plywood over and continue drilling from the other side, thus ensuring that the waste comes away in the form of a neat disc.

When the drilling is complete, the plywood has a pattern of nine equal-sized holes bored right through. In case there are any rough edges within these holes, rub inside each one with a piece of fine-grade sandpaper wrapped around a finger.

Mix a quantity of wood glue and apply it by brush to the underside of the plywood and to the rough surface of the hardboard, except in the area of the nine holes, which, of course, have not been bored in the hardboard. Bring the plywood into contact with the hardboard and keep the two surfaces pressed firmly together by weighting them down with a heavy block. The reason for taking such trouble with the application of the glue is to avoid the possibility of having it collect at the bottom of the holes.

Once the glue has dried thoroughly, remove the heavy weight and examine the combined plywood and hardboard. Now that they are joined permanently together, you may notice that their edges are not in perfect alignment. If this is the case, place the assembly in the workbench vice, the offending edge uppermost and carefully plane it down with the smoothing plane.

The eight pins, or skittles, are cut from 16mm (⅝in)-diameter dowelling each measuring 63mm (2½in) in length. Although proper skittles are shaped on a lathe and have a highly-characteristic appearance, the pins for this particular table-top game remain in the form of plain solid cylinders, their ends cut square.

There are two methods of cutting a piece of dowelling absolutely square.

The first of these is to mark the place on the dowel where it is to be cut, and then wrap a piece of straight-edged paper or thin card around the wood in such a manner that both ends of the paper overlap perfectly, indicating that the whole of the line is perpendicular to the length of the dowelling. Run the tip of a pencil around the wood, working it against the edge of the paper. Now remove the paper, lay the dowelling flat on the workbench so that its end overhangs at the side, and carefully cut along the pencil line with the hacksaw, slowly rotating the dowel until a saw-cut has been made around

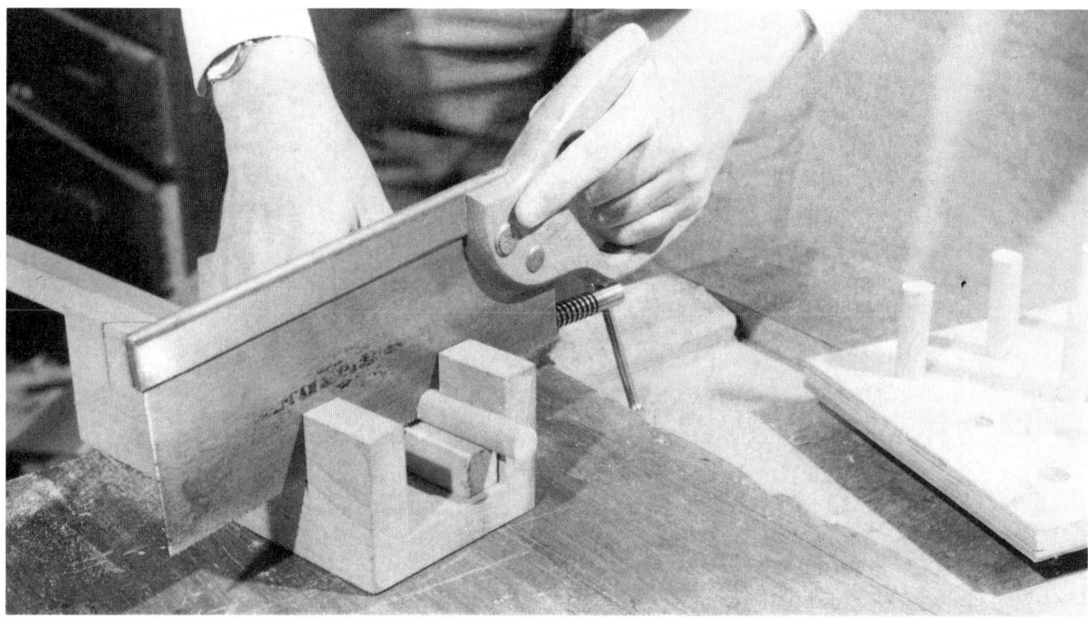

Cut the eight skittles to length, placing the dowel material in a mitre-box and cutting it absolutely square with the tenon saw.

the entire circumference. Keep sawing and turning the dowel, and eventually the waste will drop off leaving a square end. If a small piece of dowel is left projecting at the centre, trim it off with the chisel.

For the second method, mark the position on the dowel where it is to be cut, and holding it firmly in the bench-hook or the mitre-box, where it can be cut absolutely square with the tenon saw, again pause frequently to turn the dowel around so that the saw-cuts follow a line around the entire circumference.

Measure and mark the post from a piece of 16mm (⅝in)-diameter dowelling, which should be 300mm (11 13/16in) in length. The bottom end must be cut square, so that it locates fully in one of the holes prepared in the board; the top end, initially cut square, is rounded off by paring away the curved edge with the chisel and rubbing down with medium-grade sandpaper, leaving a small flat circle in the middle.

The post, because of its length and the fact that the ball swings at the end of it, must fit fully into its receiver hole in the board and, therefore, one of the corner holes – it does not matter which one – is kept to a full depth of 13mm (½in).

Having selected this one hole for the post, the remaining eight holes are partially filled in so that when the pegs are fitted into them, they can be knocked out by the whirling ball. A depth of 2mm (3/32in) is quite adequate to serve as a housing for each skittle, and this is achieved by cutting eight pieces of 16mm (⅝in)-diameter dowelling to a length of 11mm (7/16in), and gluing them into the holes, pushing them right down until

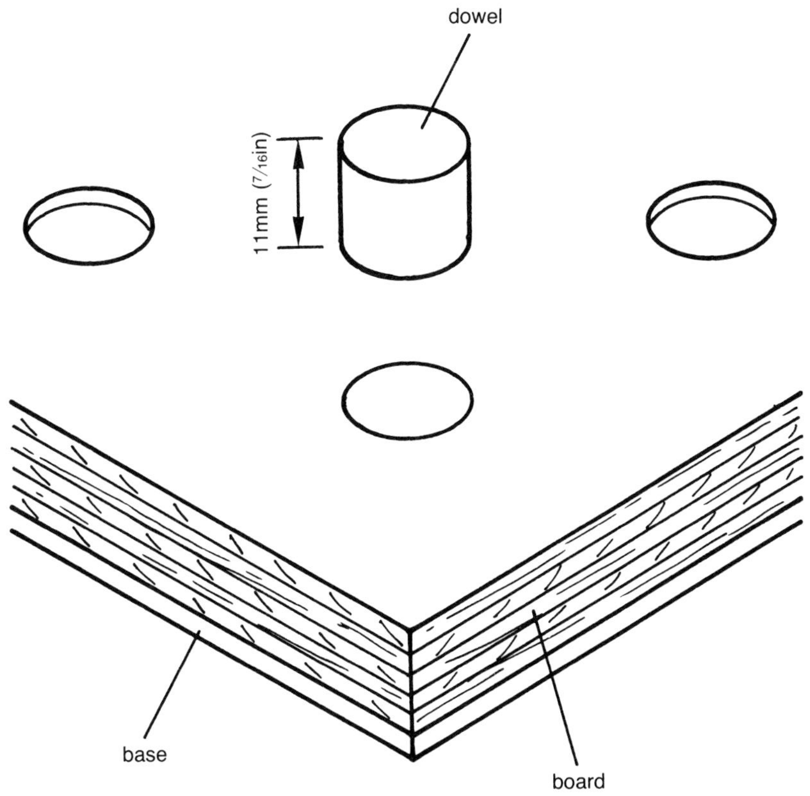

Fitting dowel into hole in board.

they make contact with the hardboard base, leaving a neat recess of 2mm (3⁄32in).

The ball is attached to the post by means of a length of string, and the string must be free to turn easily around the post at the top. The ball itself is a wooden bead of 30mm (3⁄16) diameter, which has a 9mm (3⁄8in)-diameter hole already drilled through the centre to serve some other purpose in the realms of craftwork. Plug this hole by gluing a piece of 9mm (3⁄8in)-diameter dowelling right through it and trimming the ends flat. Into one of these ends, fit a small screw-eye to which the string may be tied.

The bearing at the top of the post is made from another wooden bead, this time of 9mm (3⁄8in)-diameter or thereabouts, which should have one hole drilled right through it to accept a 25mm (1in)-long roundheaded nail used to attach it to the top of the post, and another hole of 2mm (3⁄32in) diameter, which is drilled perpendicularly through the centre, through which the string is passed. Simply thread the string through the bead, hold the bead at the top of the

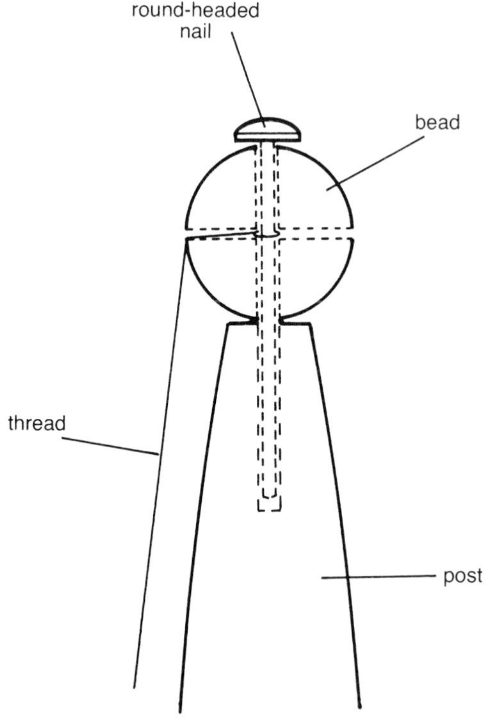

Method of attaching thread to bead and bead to post.

post and adjust the length of string so that the wooden ball is 19mm (3/4in) clear of the board, then drive the nail through the other hole, in such a way that it passes through the string and tap it well down into the post. Tie a securing knot in the end of the string next to the bead.

It now only remains to paint the outfit. The colour scheme adopted for this example is black for the board and the post and a range of bright colours for the skittles, the ball and the bead.

Cutting List

Board: one of 200×200×13mm (7 7/8×7 7/8×1/2in)
Base: one of 200×200×4mm (7 7/8×7 7/8×3/16in)
Post: one of 300×16mm (11 13/16×5/8in) diameter
Skittle: eight of 63×16mm (2 1/2×5/8in) diameter
Ball: one of 30mm (3/16in) diameter
Bead: one of 9mm (3/8in) diameter

Chapter Three

The Acrobatic Moon

This simple toy works on the principle that the moving part is pivoted about its centre of gravity so that it can perform rotations along a pair of parallel support bars, each of which has a notch cut at both ends to prevent the moving part from falling off.

The rotating part can assume any appearance that you wish. It could be the figure of a gymnast, an animal such as a monkey, or even a bird like a parrot. This example is an acrobatic moon.

The first step is to make the support bars. The size, of course, is entirely arbitrary, because you could make it as large or small as you want. However, as it is intended to amuse a fairly young child, there is little point in making it too big

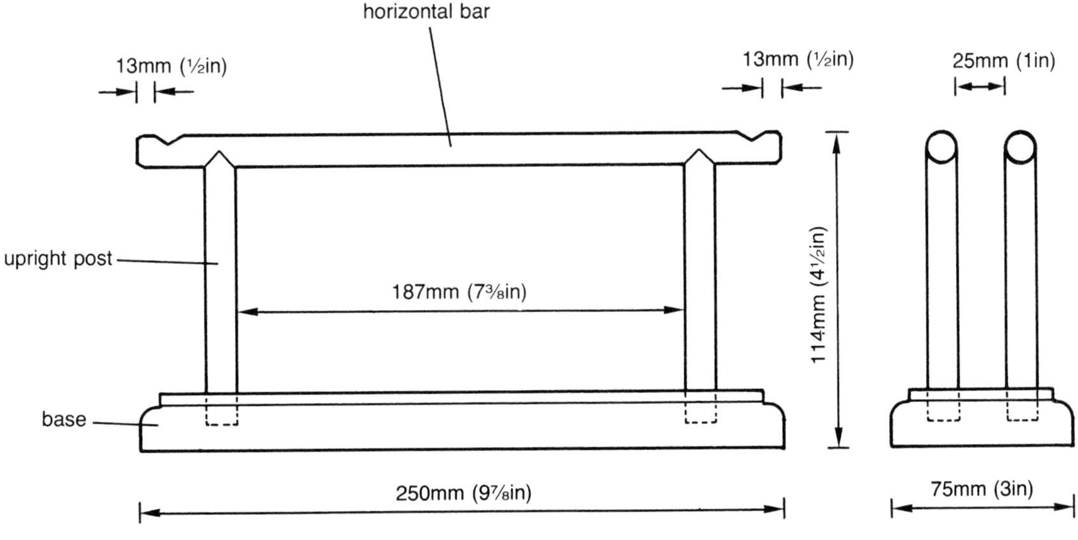

Main dimensions of the stand.

Prepare the edge-moulding on the base using the electric router fitted with a suitable cutter.

and the illustrated size is probably the most suitable.

The two parallel bars and the four vertical posts are all cut from 13mm (½in)-diameter hardwood dowelling, and the base may be prepared from any piece of hardwood. The colour and texture of the wood do not really matter, as the toy will be painted, and you will, perhaps, find a piece of left-over material in the waste bin. Preferably the wood should be of a reasonably fine grain so that a decorative pattern can be worked successfully along both the edges and endgrains. If there were a choice, beech or ramin is the best.

Start by taking the piece of material for the base, which should be cut slightly wider than you need, measure and mark it to length and cut the ends absolutely square.

The decorative edge pattern is best applied with an electric router fitted with an appropriate cutter, but if you do not own one of these tools, you could use either a plough plane or ordinary smoothing plane to give the desired effect. The plough plane is a specialised handtool that requires skilful manipulation to achieve a variety of profiles, whereas the simpler smoothing plane can be used either to bevel or chamfer the edges and end-grains, or even attempt a rounded thumbnail moulding.

Why cut the piece of wood for the base wider than necessary? Because when you work a plane or router along the end-grain, that is to say at right-angles to the direction of the grain, there is a tendency for the wood to split at the further corner. Thus, the two end-grains are prepared first and then the piece is reduced in width with the plane to remove the split ends. When the width has been brought down to the required dimension, the two remaining edges are worked with the router or the plane.

The base is now complete and is ready to be measured and marked for the four holes for the upright posts that support the two parallel bars. These must be marked very accurately, otherwise the two horizontal bars may not be perfectly parallel, and the movement of the toy will be spoilt.

For greatest accuracy, the following procedure should be used. Mark a faint pencil line on the upper surface of the base, along its length, exactly halfway between the two long edges, effectively dividing the piece into two equal halves. Now working the tape measure from each end-grain in turn, mark a point that is set in by 25mm (1in) from the two ends and square across the base in both instances. The gap between the two parallel bars is 25mm (1in), giving a distance of 12.5mm (½in) each side of the central line. However, to this amount must be added a total distance of 19mm (¾in).

Measure this 19mm (¾in) distance on each side of the line at both ends of the base to indicate where the four holes should be drilled to receive the upright posts.

Mark the positions of the four upright posts in the base, and drill them to a depth of 9mm (⅜in).

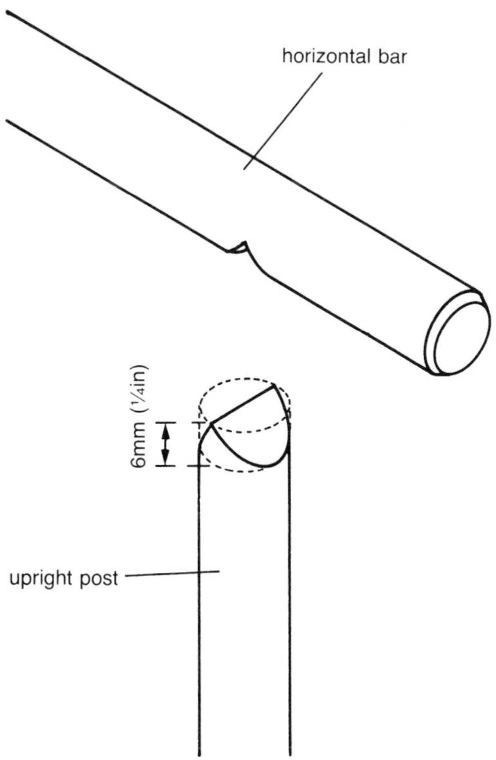

Jointing horizontal bar to upright post.

Cut an inverted V shape with a chisel at the upper end of each post, to fit notches prepared in the bars.

Fit the posts into the base, ensuring that the shaped top ends are correctly aligned.

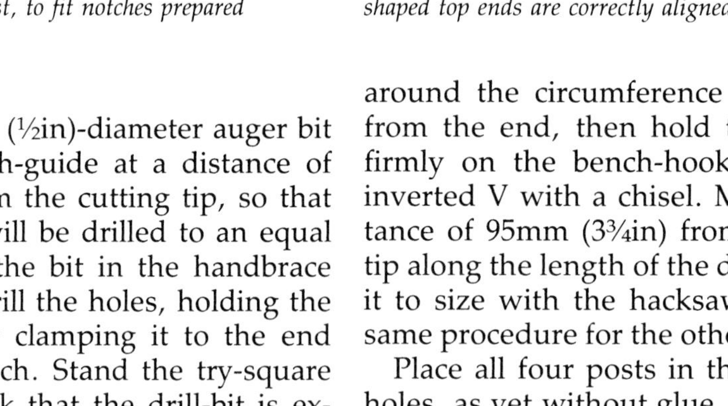

Take a 13mm (½in)-diameter auger bit and set a depth-guide at a distance of 9mm (⅜in) from the cutting tip, so that all four holes will be drilled to an equal depth. Mount the bit in the handbrace and carefully drill the holes, holding the brace firmly by clamping it to the end of the workbench. Stand the try-square upright to check that the drill-bit is exactly perpendicular to the surface of the base.

Before measuring and cutting the upright posts to length, note that they are notched into the underside of the two parallel bars, in an inverted V fashion. The notches in the bars are cut to a depth of 6.5mm (¼in) or half of the bars' diameter and the top of each post is correspondingly shaped to fit.

Start by trimming the posts. Taking a long piece of 13mm (½in)-diameter dowelling material, mark off a pencil around the circumference 6.5mm (¼in) from the end, then hold the dowelling firmly on the bench-hook and cut the inverted V with a chisel. Measure a distance of 95mm (3¾in) from the pointed tip along the length of the dowel, and cut it to size with the hacksaw. Repeat the same procedure for the other three posts.

Place all four posts in their respective holes, as yet without glue, to check for a satisfactory fitting.

Cut the two horizontal bars to the same length as the base, rounding off their ends by rubbing lightly with fine-grade sandpaper. Mark in the position of the notches, each one being set in 25mm (1in) from the end. Taking each bar in turn, clamp it flat on the end of the workbench, with a piece of soft cloth packed in between to protect the surface of the dowelling, and saw down halfway through the diameter in both the marked positions with the hacksaw – this tool is

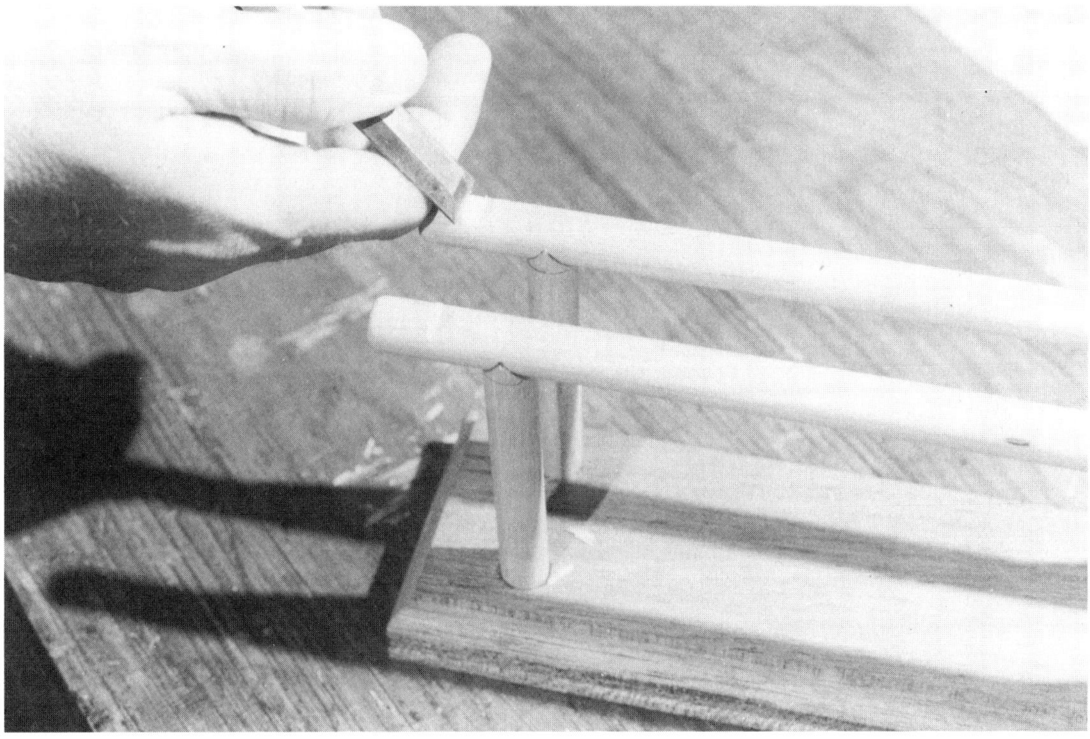

End-stop notches are cut with the hacksaw and chisel near to the ends of each bar.

preferable to the tenon saw because it has a much narrower blade.

Carefully cut a V-shaped notch with the chisel, matching precisely with the pointed tips prepared at the end of each post. Finally, turn the bars through 180 degrees and cut shallower notches 13mm (½in) from the ends to act as a stop for the rotating figure. These secondary notches need only be cut to a depth of 4mm (3/16in) or so.

Check that the two parallel bars fit properly on to their posts and when you are satisfied that they are both level and upright, mix a small amount of wood glue and apply it to all the joining surfaces, leaving the assembly to dry thoroughly.

We now come to the making of the rotating part – in this case, the acrobatic moon. The moon, of course, is cut in a crescent shape and is given a prominent nose and a nice smiling face. Start by marking out a template on a piece of thick card. Set a pair of geometrical compasses to a radius of 75mm (3in) and draw a circle. Roughly sketch out how you want the face to look, and draw in the lines using a set of artist's French curves. Although the details of the face, such as the eye, eye-brow and mouth, do not really matter at this stage, it is still a good idea to add them to the template so that you can judge the overall effect.

Cut out the card template using a sharp knife, taking care to follow the curves precisely.

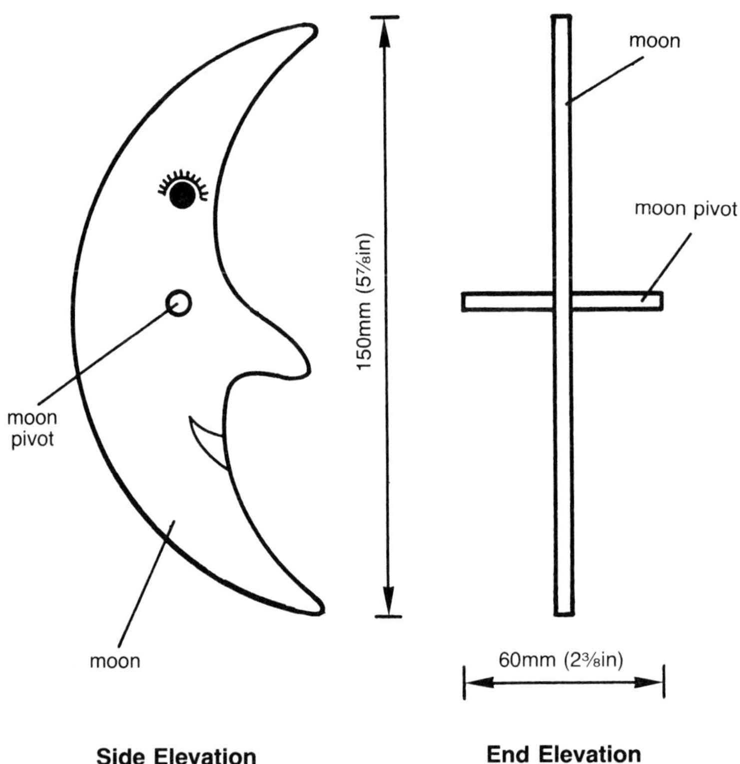

Main dimensions of moon.

The next step is to find the position of the pivot, which must be located at the centre of rotation, the point where all the forces acting on the figure are balanced. It is important to get this right, otherwise the moon will not rotate freely along the bars.

Finding the centre of rotation is initially something of a guess but you can see from the illustrations roughly where it should be. Take a long sewing needle and poke it through the card so that an equal amount of needle projects from either side. Now rest the template on the parallel bars and see if it has a tendency to rotate of its own accord, indicating that the needle is off balance from the true centre of rotation. Make further tests until the template is properly balanced. Make a note of the appropriate needle hole by circling it in pencil and take the needle out.

Transfer the outline *precisely* on to a piece of 9mm (⅜in)-thick birch-faced plywood, which has a very smooth-textured surface, and cut around the pencil line with the coping saw, working the blade just to the waste side of the line and tak-

Mark the crescent moon on a card template, using a pair of compasses, French curves and a pencil. The eye and mouth are drawn in simply to judge their effect.

ing great care not to break off splinters.

Rub down the sawn edges to the pencil line, first using a medium-grade sandpaper and then fine-grade. Check that the plywood figure still matches the shape of the template – if anything, it would be preferable for the plywood to be cut slightly too large, because it can easily be reduced with further sandpapering.

Mark the centre of rotation on the side of the plywood moon by pressing the point of the bradawl through the correct needle hole in the template and drill through the ply with a 6mm-diameter twist drill, taking the usual precautions to prevent the wood from splitting on the underside.

Cut a 60mm (2⅜in) length of 6mm (¼in)-diameter dowelling, round off the ends with fine-grade sandpaper and glue

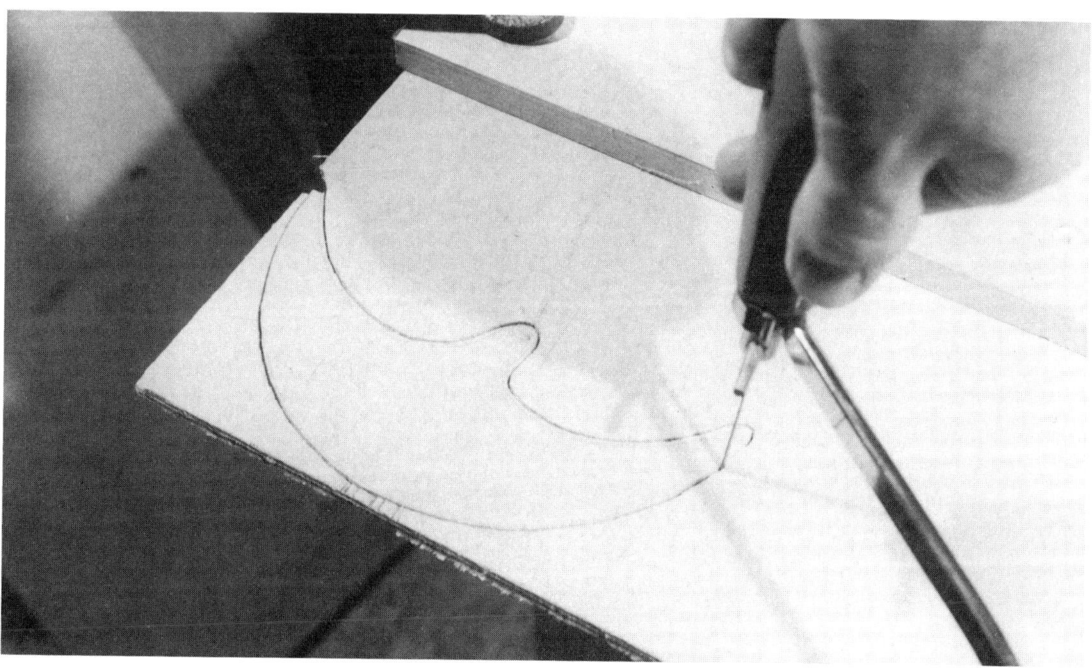

Cut around the outline of the moon with the coping saw.

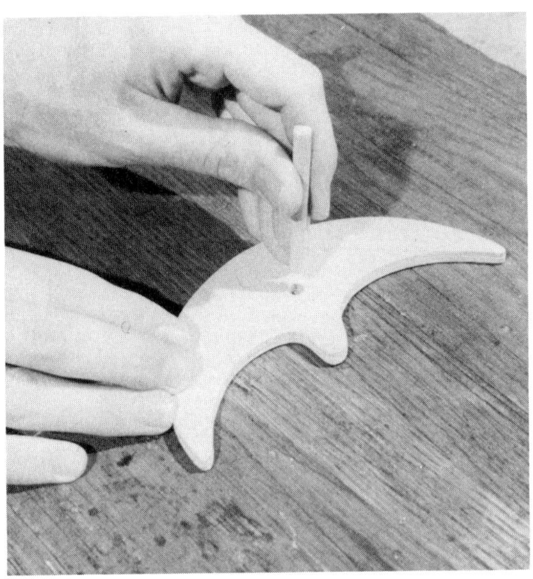

Find the moon's centre of rotation, drill a hole through at that point, and fit the pivot.

it into the hole drilled through the moon so that an equal length projects at either side.

When the glue has dried thoroughly, paint the moon and the stand in a colour scheme of your own choice, add the face details to the moon and the toy is finished and ready to go for a spin.

Cutting List

Moon: one of 150×70×9mm (5⅞×2¾×⅜in)
Base: one of 250×75×22mm (9⅞×3×⅞in)
Horizontal bar: two of 250×13mm (9⅞×½in) diameter
Upright post: four of 95×13mm (3¾×½in) diameter
Moon pivot: one of 60×6mm (2⅜×¼in) diameter

CHAPTER FOUR

THE CLOCK PUZZLE

The clock puzzle is a learning toy with three purposes: it helps the young child acquire manual dexterity, as all puzzles do; but it also teaches the child to count from one to twelve and, when the clock hands are fitted in place, assists in learning to tell the time.

The puzzle is of simple construction. There is an outer ring of plywood into which the twelve separate numbers fit, and, at the centre, is a circular boss with a hole drilled through it to receive the clock's two hands. The outer ring and the centre boss are both fixed on to a hardboard backing panel, which has a series of holes drilled through it to accept small dowel pegs glued to the back of each number segment. The holes, two per segment, are arranged partly in a spiral pattern, so that each of the twelve segments has its own particular position, thus ensuring that the numbers can only be fitted in the correct order.

The two hands are detachable, otherwise the puzzle would not be able to fit together without either one or the other getting in the way, but this also means that they may be put to one side until the child is old enough to understand their significance.

Take a square piece of 6mm (¼in)-thick birch-faced plywood and mark two circles on it for the outer ring, using a pair of geometrical compasses. This outside ring has an outer diameter of 250mm (9⅞in) and an inner diameter of 210mm (8¼in). At the same time, take a matching square piece of hardboard, measuring 3mm (⅛in) in thickness, and mark the inner diameter 210mm (8¼in) on the rough surface.

In both cases, note where the point of the compasses has made an impression, and mark the position clearly by circling it with a pencil. It is important to get the position correct for both the plywood and the hardboard.

The next step is to cut out the middle of the plywood just to the waste side of the inner circumference, that is to say, the line of 210mm (8¼in) diameter. The best way of doing this is by cutting away the unwanted waste portion using the electric router.

First, fit the router with an attachment plate that enables the tool to describe a perfect circle of any chosen diameter. The plate has a small hole drilled through it which acts as the pivot. Mount a rebate cutter of 6mm (¼in)-diameter in the router, place the plywood on a large piece of flat scrap wood, and drive a nail through the pivot hole in the attachment plate so that the point of it passes precisely through the centre of the 210mm (8¼in)-diameter circle. Hammer the nail right

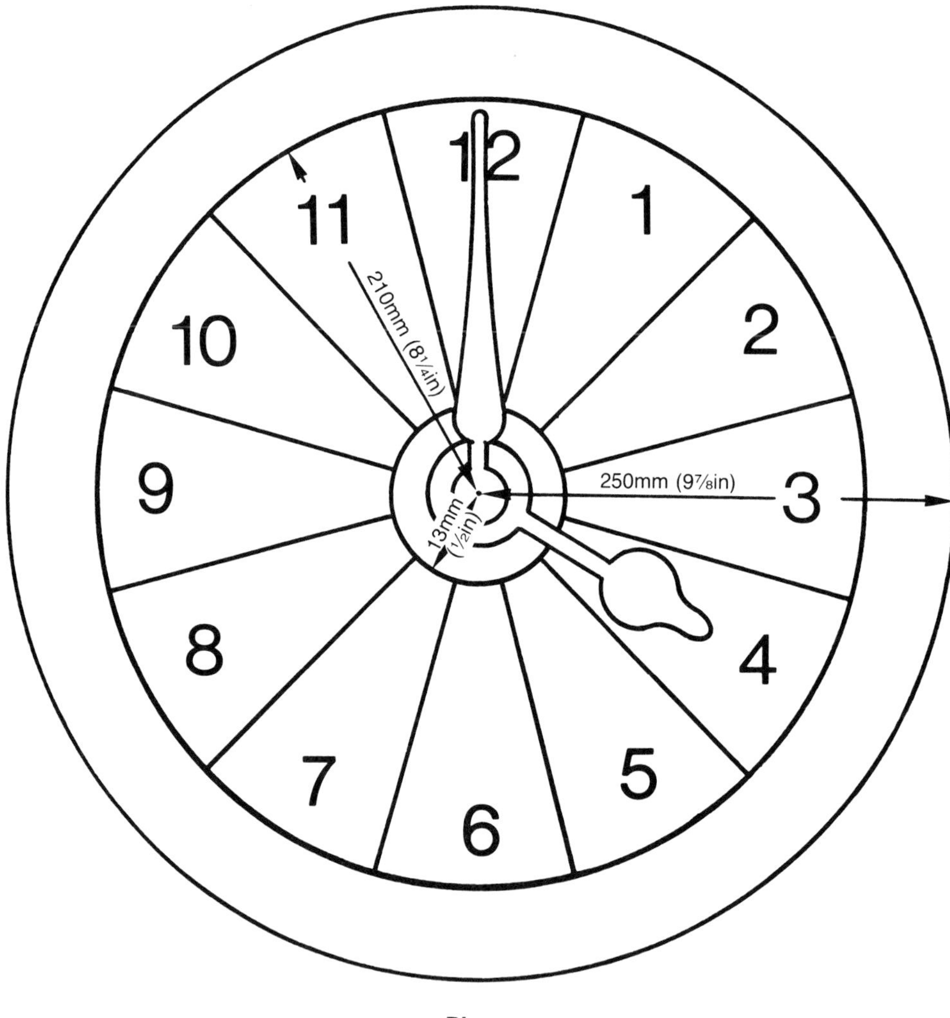

Main dimensions of the clock puzzle.

through into the scrap wood and clamp the plywood to the backing board in at least two places. Remember that the plywood is still cut in the form of a square panel.

Adjust the position of the router with respect to the attachment plate until the rebating cutter just makes contact with the pencilled circle, cutting on the waste side. Lock the router firmly in this position and make the first circular cut to a depth of 2mm (3/32in) or so, taking care not to push the router too fast so that it makes a clean cut. Apply further downward pressure and repeat the same process, making a second circular cut to a depth of about 4mm (3/16in).

Withdraw the nail from the pivot hole, undo the two clamps holding the plywood to the backing board, and turn it

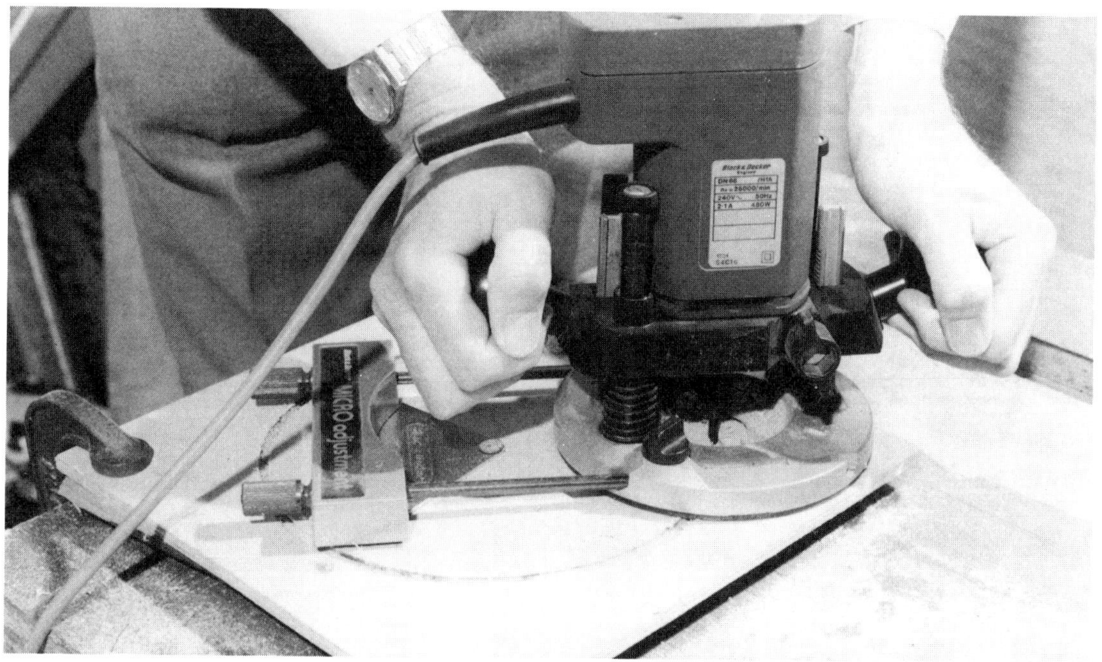

Cut a circle out of the plywood to make the outer frame, using the router and fixing its centre of rotation to the middle of the panel with a flat-headed nail.

over, re-fastening the clamps and driving the nail back through the same hole. Make the third and final cut from the opposite side so that the rebating meets within the thickness of the plywood, thus eliminating the likelihood of splintering the surface.

When the waste has been removed, you are left with the original square of plywood with a 210mm (8¼in)-diameter circle cut out of the centre. The square of plywood must now be stuck on to the hardboard in such a position that the cut-out circle coincides exactly with the 210mm (8¼in)-diameter circle described on the rough surface of the hardboard.

Mix a quantity of wood glue and apply it by brush to the hardboard surface and the underside of the plywood. Assemble the plywood to the hardboard, and press

Glue the clock frame, with the circular centre portion removed, to the hardboard backing panel.

them firmly together while the glue dries and hardens. The best way to do this is to lay the assembly flat on the workbench, place the large scrap board on top and weight it down with several bricks or concrete blocks.

Now prepare the small centre boss to which the clock's hands will be fitted. This is made from the same 6mm (¼in)-thickness plywood and has a diameter of 25mm (1in). It may be marked out and cut from the piece of waste taken out from the middle of the clock. However, it is much more difficult to cut a small disc of wood using the router method, and you may find it more satisfactory to cut around the marked circle with the coping saw and sandpaper the edge to a perfect circle.

Locate the boss in position on the hardboard by pushing the nail through the hole in its centre and lining this up with the small pin-point impression left on the surface of the hardboard by the pair of compasses. Mix a small amount of wood glue and assemble the boss, taking care to avoid letting any glue squeeze out on to the hardboard. Keep the boss pressed firmly to the hardboard as the glue dries.

When the boss is fitted in place on the backing panel, attach the router so that it pivots about the centre of the clock, and cut the outer frame to size.

Locate the boss in position on the backing panel, using a nail to set it exactly in the centre, and fix with glue.

Cut off the unwanted waste from the outer part of the clock, along the 250mm (9⅞in)-diameter line, using the same method as before; setting up the router on its attachment plate, which is pivotted through the boss, clamping the plywood-and-hardboard combination on to a large board of scrap material, and adjusting the position of the router cutter so that it just touches on the outside of the pencilled circle. Make two passes of the router from this side, increasing the depth of the cut, before turning it over to make

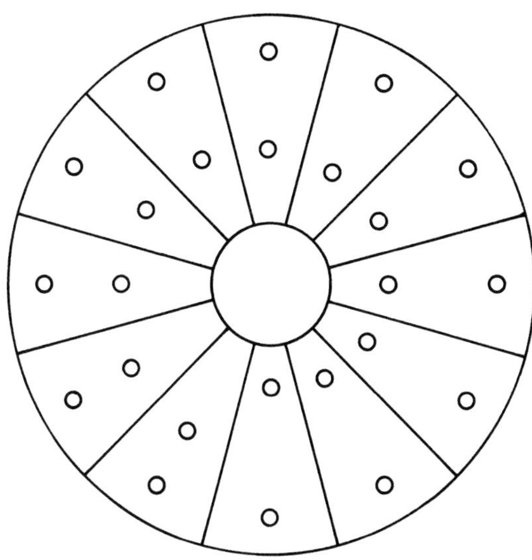

Positions of the twenty-four peg holes marked in the plywood that will become the twelve segments of the clock-face. Note how the inner holes form a spiral pattern.

Lay the marked-out card template inside the recessed clock, and punch a small hole through each of the twenty-four peg positions with a panel pin and hammer.

the third cut directly on to the hardboard, removing the outer portion of waste. Lightly sandpaper the outside edge of the clock.

The next step is to mark and drill out the holes for the fixing pegs in the hardboard. This should be done with great precision. Start by marking out a card template, identical in size to the recess, with an outer diameter of 210mm (8¼in) and an inner diameter of 25mm (1in). Before cutting it to fit, mark off 30 divisions from the centre using a geometrical protractor to indicate the twelve equal divisions between the numerals on the clock-face, then measure and mark in the positions of the peg-holes, as shown in the illustration.

Cut out the template to fit into the hardboard recess and, using a panel pin and a light hammer, punch a small hole

Remove the template and drill through the backing panel with a 6mm (¼in) diameter auger bit in the twenty-four peg positions.

through each of the twenty-four peg positions. Remove the template, and drill down into each of the pilot-holes with a 6mm (¼in)-diameter auger bit, boring right through the hardboard. So that each hole is drilled cleanly through the material, the clock should be clamped firmly to a piece of scrap wood. Note how the inner holes form the required spiral pattern.

To make the twelve segments for the puzzle, copy the dimensions of the card template on to a piece of 6mm (¼in)-thick birch-faced plywood and cut off the waste from both the outer and the inner edges using the electric router with the pivoting attachment plate. This time, position the router cutter exactly on the two pencilled circles to ensure that the finished disc fits into the recess without binding, otherwise the child will have difficulty fitting the pieces in properly and consequently lose interest.

Before cutting the disc up into twelve equal segments, fit it into the recess so that it makes contact with the hardboard of the base, and clamp it to prevent it from turning or coming out. Lie the clock face downwards on the workbench, that is to say with the shiny surface of the hardboard uppermost and, using the 6mm (¼in)-diameter auger bit mounted in the handbrace, bore down through each of the twenty-four peg-holes until the tip of the drill-bit *just* begins to make an impression on the opposite side of the disc. This will effectively mean that you have drilled approximately 3mm (⅛in) deep into the plywood.

Remove the disc and mark out the twelve divisions on the surface in which the peg-holes have been drilled, arranging for the lines to be drawn exactly midway between each successive pair of holes. Cut the disc into twelve separate segments with the hacksaw, taking care to follow each line precisely. The hacksaw is preferable to either the jig-saw or the tenon saw because its blade is much narrower and, therefore, there will be less kerf so that the assembled puzzle pieces will sit closer together. The one disadvantage of using the hacksaw is that the direction of the cut can wander off the straight line.

Rub down the edges of each segment with fine-grade sandpaper to remove thin strands of wood.

Cut twenty-four pieces of 6mm (¼in)-diameter dowelling, each 6mm (¼in) in length, making sure that their ends are

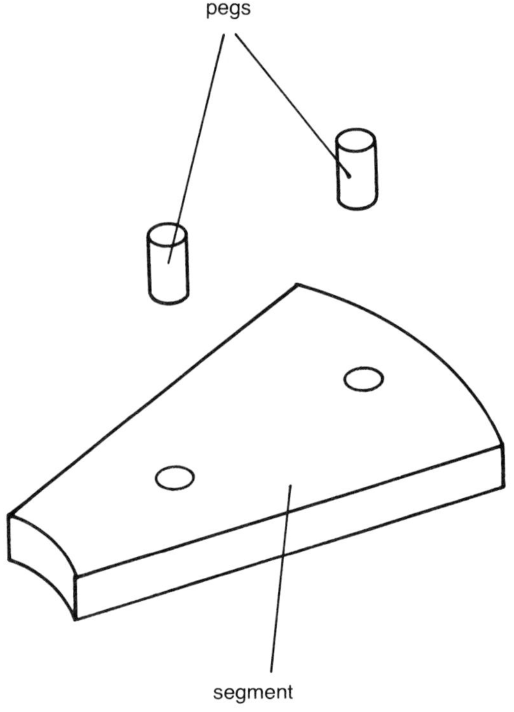

The dowel pegs are fitted into each of the twelve segments.

perfectly square, then mix some wood glue and with a brush apply a little to each of the peg-holes, pushing the dowels fully into place and wiping away any excess glue.

When the glue is completely dry, fit all twelve segments into their correct positions on the clock-face. Rub down the surface with fine-grade sandpaper until it is smooth to the touch.

How you approach the question of applying the numbers one to twelve on the twelve segments depends on your skill as an artist: ideally, they should be painted on in bright colours, perhaps with other artistic touches, such as the painting of small nursery-rhyme characters, to add more interest. But if this is beyond your capability, use stick-on transfers to build up a picture; this jig-saw puzzle effect will help the child fit the pieces back in the correct order.

Whatever sort of illustration you opt to put on the clock-face, firstly remove all twelve segments before giving each one, and the plywood frame, an application of undercoat before painting in bright colours.

The final stage is to make the clock's hands. The short hour hand is fixed onto a length of 16mm (⅝in)-diameter dowelling, which has a 6mm (¼in)-diameter hole bored through the middle to receive a length of 6mm (¼in)-diameter dowelling on to which the long minute hand is attached. This arrangement, seemingly complicated but actually quite straightforward, permits the two hands to rotate freely and independently of one another, so that they can be set to indicate any

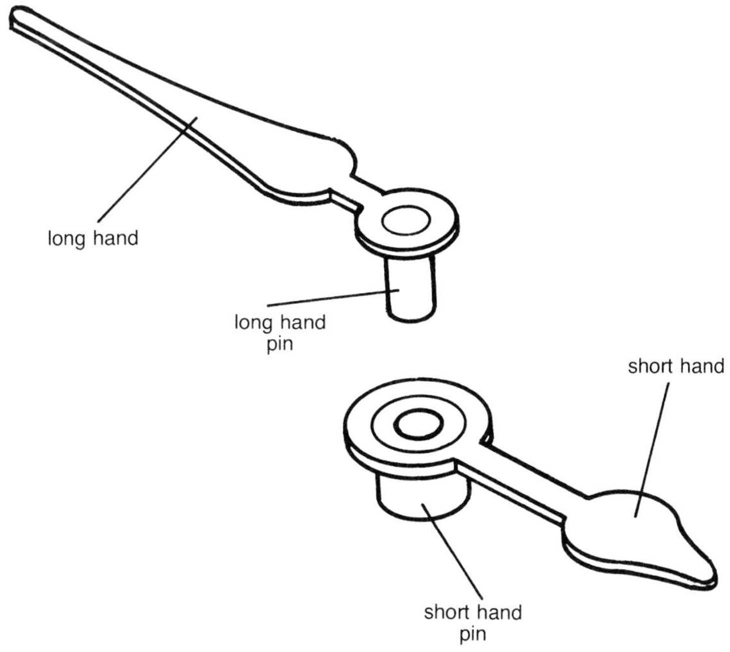

Fitting the hands together.

desired time. They can also be fitted into and taken out of the clock-face quickly and easily.

Mark both the hands on to a piece of 3mm (⅛in)-thick birch-faced plywood, noting that they should not be too pointed at their ends, but rounded for safety. The long hand measures 100mm (4in) in length, and the short hand 75mm (3in) from the tip to the point at the centre of the clock about which they both turn. However, at this point the short hand has a circle of 12.5mm (½in) radius marked, and the long hand a circle of 8mm (5⁄16in) radius. At the centre of each of these circles, a hole is drilled out – for the short hand the hole is made with a 16mm (⅝in)-diameter bit and for the long hand, the hole is made with a 6mm (¼in)-diameter bit.

Complete the marking out of the pattern for both the hands, then cut around each one with the coping saw, working it carefully to avoid splintering the plies. Rub down the two hands with medium-grade and then fine-grade sandpaper to round off the edges.

Now take the 16mm (⅝in)-diameter centre bit, mounted in the handbrace, place the tip of the bit at the centre of the boss and drill right through the combined plywood and hardboard.

Cut the end of a piece of 16mm (⅝in)-diameter dowelling perfectly square, measure and mark its centre and, with the dowelling clamped upright in the vice, drill down into it with the 6mm (¼in)-diameter auger bit to a depth exceeding 16mm (⅝in). Mark off a point 13mm (½in) from the end and cut the dowel to this length.

Similarly, take a piece of 6mm (¼in)-diameter dowelling, square off the end, and cut a piece measuring 16mm (⅝in) long. Mix a small amount of wood glue and apply it by brush to the holes drilled through the two hands. Into the 16mm (⅝in)-diameter hole drilled in the short hand, fit one end of the 16mm (⅝in)-diameter dowel, and into the 6mm (¼in)-diameter hole drilled in the long hand, fit one end of the 6mm (¼in)-diameter dowel. When the glue has dried completely give the hands a coat of matt black paint.

The dowel of the long hand fits into the dowel of the short hand and both of these fit into the hole drilled in the boss at the centre of the clock.

Cutting List

Clock frame: one of 280×280×6mm (11×11×¼in)
Backing panel: one of 280×280×4mm (11×11×3⁄16in)
Numeral segments: one of 240×240×6mm (9½×9½×¼in)
Long hand: one of 100×16×3mm (4×⅝×⅛in)
Short hand: 75×25×3mm (3×1×⅛in)
Long hand pin: one of 16×6mm (⅝×¼in) diameter
Short hand pin: one of 13×16mm (½×⅝in) diameter
Puzzle peg: twenty-four of 6×6mm (¼×¼in) diameter

Chapter Five

The Pull-Along Duck

The duck-on-wheels is a simple-to-make toy that will appeal to very young children who always seem to enjoy picking up a string and pulling a small animal along behind them.

Two features are important: firstly, because toddlers are impetuous in the way they handle their toys, the duck should be low and squat, with the wheels set wide apart for greater stability, so that even with hard tugs and sudden changes in direction, it remains upright most of the time. The second characteristic is that it ought to do something apart from merely roll along the floor – so why not bob up and down as well? The front wheels are off-set to rotate in an eccentric movement, causing the duck to move up and down, as real ducks do when they swim on water.

The duck is made in three parts, consisting of the body and two folded wings that are tucked against its sides. The type of wood might at first seem unimportant

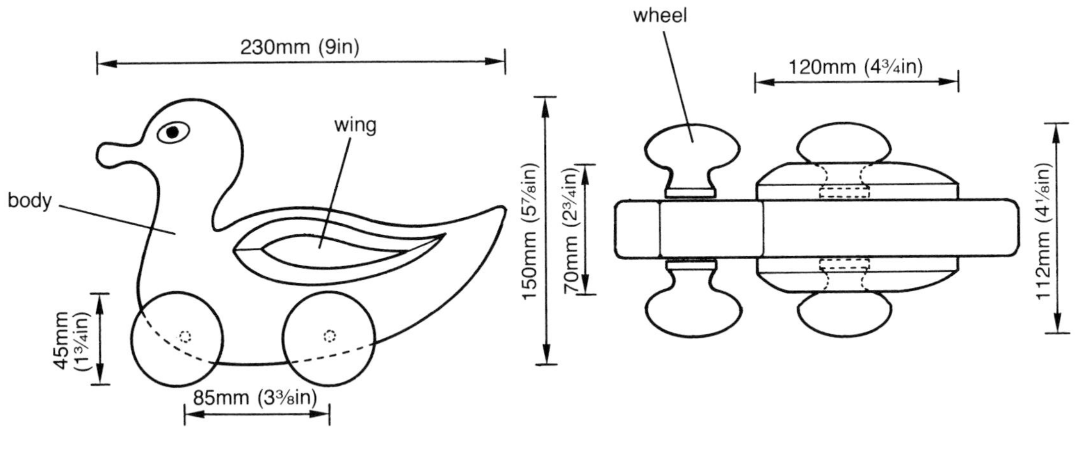

Main dimensions of the duck.

if the duck is to be painted anyway but, of course, that is not the whole story. Though perfectly simple in design, this project involves a great deal of shaping, and it is sensible to select a wood that responds favourably to the coping saw, the spokeshave and the chisel.

The illustrated duck is made from parana pine which is a virtually knot-free softwood, evenly-grained and fairly dense. An alternative might be the hardwood beech. As very little material is needed, it will certainly pay to sort through all the left-over bits in the waste-bin.

DRAWING AND CUTTING OUT

Start by preparing a card template. With any shaped piece of woodwork, a template is an important opening stage, because this is the only time when the shaping can be altered without the risk of making a bad cut and wasting wood. In particular, avoid drawing the beak too small, otherwise the finished result could break off and cause jagged splinters.

The outline of the duck should be sketched lightly freehand before drawing in the final shape with French curves and a pair of compasses. The dimensions of the duck's body are approximately 230mm (9in) long and 150mm (5⅞in) high to the top of the head, the wood from which it is cut being 32mm (1¼in) thick.

Cut out the template with a sharp knife, place it on the wood with the direction of the wood grain running from the front of the duck's body to its tail, and draw around it in pencil. The cutting out will be made easier and somewhat more precise if you mark an identical outline with the template reversed on the opposite side of the wood, but you must make several accurate reference marks on both sides to ensure that the two outlines correspond.

Hold the wood securely in the workbench vice and cut round the pencil lines with the coping saw, keeping the blade just to the waste side at all times. The tightest corner is the one at the back of the head where it forms the neck, and you will find that the coping saw is capable of making very sharp changes in direction, proving a better tool than the jig-saw in this particular case.

When the waste has been removed, clamp the body of the duck in the vice and, using the spokeshave, gradually plane down the remaining waste to the marked line. This tool is excellent for making smooth, sweeping curves, but you will have difficulty getting it into the back of the neck or around the duck's beak. These areas will have to be carefully filed smooth.

Mark in the positions of the two holes that receive the wheel axles. The axles are cut from 6mm (¼in)-diameter steel rod and, therefore, a 6mm (¼in)-diameter auger bit will be required to drill the holes. The distance between the two axles is 85mm (3⅜in) and each hole is set in by 13mm (½in) from the bottom edge. The hole positions should be marked on both sides of the duck, using the tape measure, square and pencil, so that the holes can be drilled from both directions to meet halfway through the thickness of the wood.

When the holes have been drilled, check that they are large enough to receive the 6mm (¼in)-diameter axle rod by pushing a length of it through. If resistance is felt, enlarge the holes with a

Mark the outline of the duck from the card template on to the wood, and cut around it with a coping saw.

Place the roughly-sawn body of the duck in the vice, and smooth the curves with the spokeshave.

Drill out the wheel axle holes with a 6mm (¼in) diameter auger bit, boring from both sides of the wood.

Shape the more awkward, tightly-curved edges of the duck body with the chisel.

rat-tail file until the axle material can be fitted right through and turned by hand.

The shaping of the duck's body can now be completed by rounding off all the edges. The long curves of the body should be shaped with the spokeshave, but the shorter curves around the head, neck and beak will need the blade of a well-sharpened chisel, carefully manipulated by hand, to shave off the unwanted square corners. Finish the rounding off with the file before rubbing down thoroughly with medium-grade and then fine-grade sandpaper.

The two wings come next. These are shaped to follow the contours on the upper part of the duck's back, and should have an aerodynamic appearance, even though they are meant to be folded. The easiest way to achieve the right shape and proportion is to draw the wing on the original card template and cut it out. Take a piece of parana pine measuring 19mm (¾in) in thickness and mark around the wing template twice to give two identical patterns, cutting these out with the coping saw.

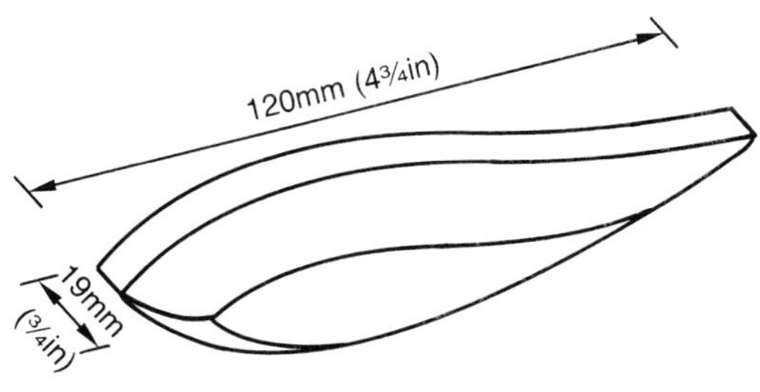

Main dimensions of the wing.

Cut out the wing shape from the main template, then mark a pair of outlines on to the wood.

Clamp the wing to the end of the workbench, and shape the edge with the spokeshave, finishing with sandpaper.

As with the duck's body, the wings must be shaped with the spokeshave, and their edges rounded off to give a smooth, flowing appearance – but, of course, you will have to take care to round off opposite sides, as one wing is to be mounted on the left side of the duck and the other on the right side.

Complete the preparation of the wings by rubbing down thoroughly with sandpaper.

Glue the wings to the body, securing with a G-clamp.

ASSEMBLY

Place each wing in position on the side of the duck, adjusting it until both are in corresponding locations, and mark around in pencil. Mix some wood glue and apply it with a small brush to the marked areas and to the inside surfaces of the wings. Butt them in place and clamp them firmly to the sides of the duck while the glue dries and sets hard. Wipe away any excess glue that squeezes out from the joints using a damp cloth.

THE WHEELS

The wheels are made from 45mm (1¾in)-diameter wooden door knobs. These are ideally suitable because the shape of the knob, being relatively deep, permits a wide-wheeled effect with the advantage of improved stability. When you purchase wooden door knobs you will usually find that they either have a screw-thread fitted in place, or the centre is drilled with a tiny pilot hole.

For the pair of knobs used to make the two back wheels, the centres should be drilled out with the 6mm (¼in)-diameter auger bit to a depth of 19mm (¾in) to receive the axle rod, which is cut to a length of 74mm (3in), thus allowing a small amount of movement between the wheels and the body. The steel rod is bonded into the holes with a powerful all-purpose adhesive.

The front wheels are treated somewhat differently. They are mounted off-centre to give the duck its up-and-down movement. From the centre of each wheel, measure 6mm (¼in) outwards and drill the axle hole at this point, boring to a depth of 19mm (¾in). When it comes to assembling the pair of wheels on the axle, they will have to be rotated until it can be seen that their eccentrics match.

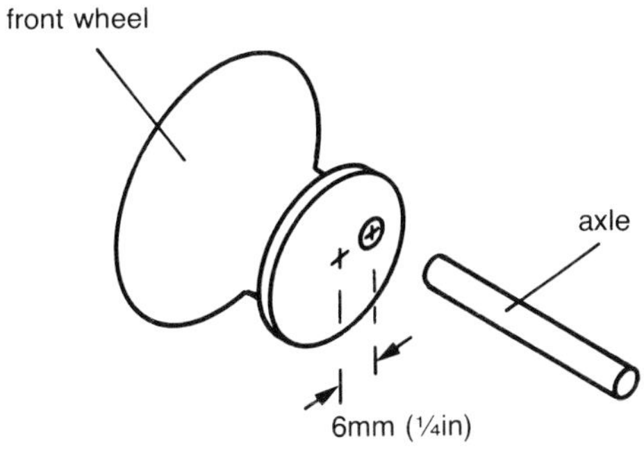

Off-centre position of the front wheel axle.

FINISHING TOUCHES

The eyes of the duck are made from felt – a large oval shape cut out from white felt and the smaller black circle from black felt – which are fixed in place with adhesive.

The pull-along cord is tied to a small picture-frame ring that screws into a small hole made in the front of the duck.

Finally, if the duck is to be painted you can choose your own colours, but it is best to use bright colours that can also be made to look reasonably realistic. The wheels should be painted in primary colours to catch the interest of the young child. Use only non-toxic paints that are safe even if the child bites the toy, because toddlers explore most things with their mouths.

Cutting List

Body: one of 230×150×32mm (9×5⅞×1¼in)
Wing: two of 120×45×19mm (4¾×1¾×¾in)
Wheel: four of 40×45mm (1 7/16×1¾in) diameter

CHAPTER SIX

THE STRING PUPPET

Although it looks quite difficult, the string puppet is not hard to make, and will give many hours of pleasure. All sorts of figures can be animated but the most popular are marionettes in costume.

This puppet is made in the form of a clown, and it is really the style of the outfit that tells you what it is rather than any distinguishing feature of the doll itself. The wooden marionette could, indeed, be dressed in a wide variety of costumes, so its final appearance is dictated by the way it is dressed, calling for as much skill in sewing as in woodwork.

To make the puppet, the first step is to shape the head and the body, and, for these, two blocks of wood are required. Both of these may be carved by hand; however, a more satisfactory result will be obtained if the two parts are turned individually in the lathe.

Unless you have a very well-equipped workshop, it is unlikely that you own a proper wood-turning lathe, but small bench-mounted lathes can be purchased very reasonably and are powered by an ordinary electric drill. They have obvious limitations and can only turn fairly small sections of wood. However, for this sort of workload they are ideal.

Only very small pieces of wood are needed and the scrap-wood bin will surely yield something suitable. Admittedly, there are preferred woods for turning, and some types give excellent results whereas others splinter badly and produce rough surfaces. Hardwoods such as as afrormosia, maple and sycamore can be considered good for lathe-work.

The illustrated example was turned from oak, which is actually not one of the best hardwoods for turning – at least not this particular variety – but, even if you cannot get hold of exactly what you want, oak usually proves a safe choice. The colour of the wood does not matter because it will be painted over.

The arms and legs are cut from a length of ramin dowelling, the arms using material of 9mm (⅜in)-diameter and the legs material of 13mm (½in)-diameter. The hands and the feet are shaped from small blocks of ramin cut from strips measuring 25×13mm (1×½in) that can be bought at any DIY shop.

THE BODY

Start by making the body. This is cut from a rectangular block measuring 105×55×28mm (4⅛×2⅛×1⅛in). Saw both of the ends perfectly square and mark in their centres by drawing two straight lines from diagonally opposed

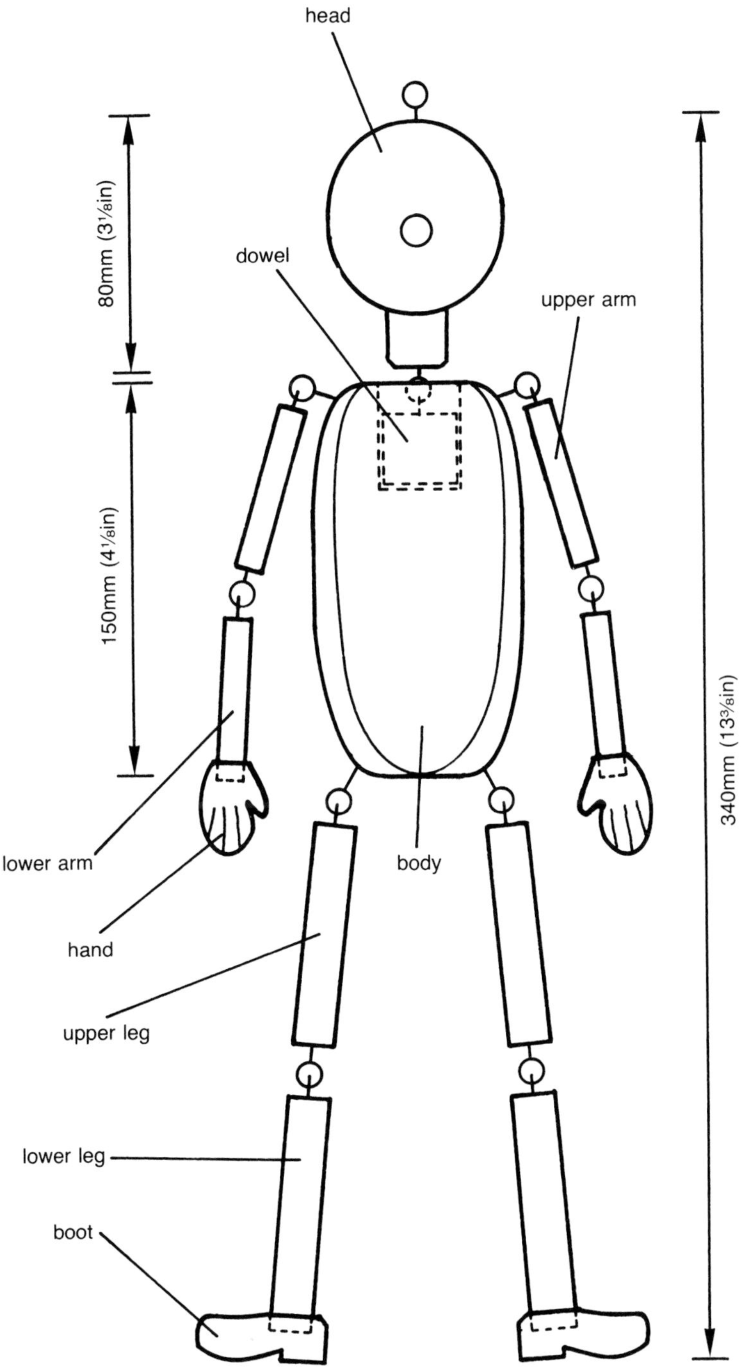

Main dimensions of the string puppet.

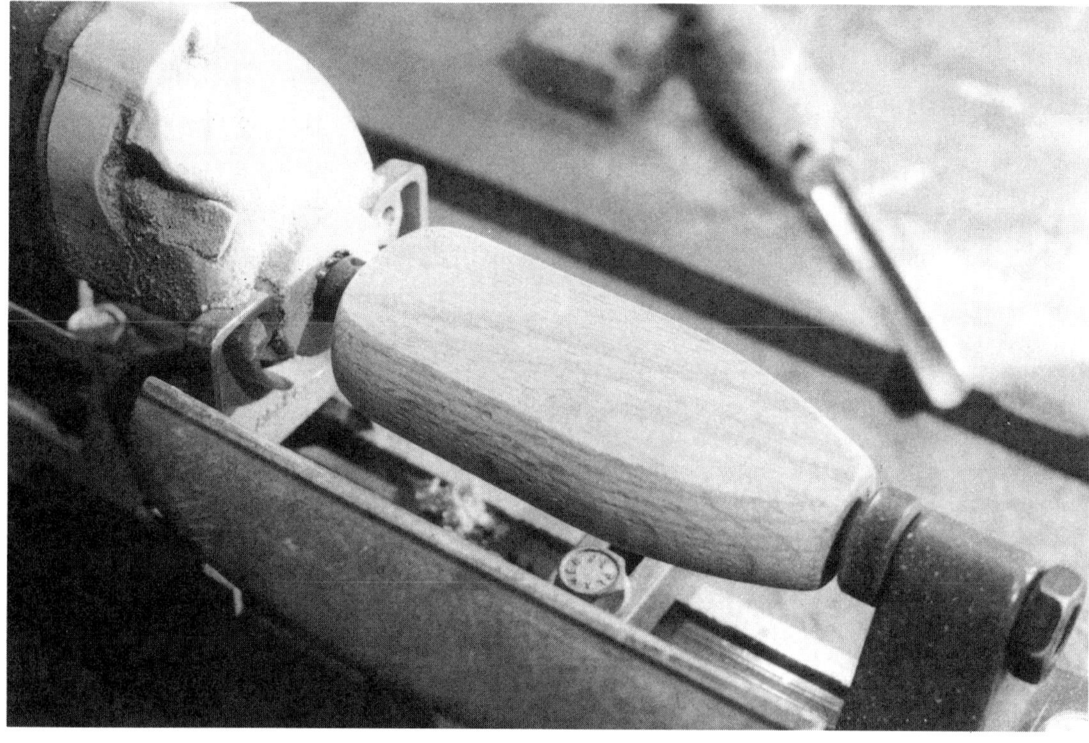

The body is essentially a long rectangular block, rounded off at the shoulders and tapered and curved towards the bottom end.

corners. The centre is at the point where the two lines cross. The headstock and tailstock of the lathe will be driven into these positions.

Before commencing to turn the body in the lathe, some of the rough shaping can be carried out with the chisel and mallet and the spokeshave. This is intended merely to round off the corners and edges so that the initial stages of woodturning do not cause the block to split.

Mount the body between the headstock and tailstock and, wearing protective spectacles to shield the eyes, rest the spindle gouge on the tool-rest, bring its cutting tip into contact with the spinning wood, gradually turning it to the desired shape. In particular, the shoulders should be properly rounded and the body tapered slightly downwards to the position where the legs will be mounted. This is not intended to be a work of art, so there is no need to be too realistic – besides, it will be dressed in a voluminous clown's outfit.

Remove the body from the lathe and place it upright in the vice, shoulders uppermost. In the position where the headstock was fixed, now shown by tell-tale marks, drill out a 19mm (¾in)-diameter hole with a centre bit mounted in a handbrace, boring to a depth of 25mm (1in). This hole is made to receive the dowel block that serves to anchor the head to the body, but more about that later.

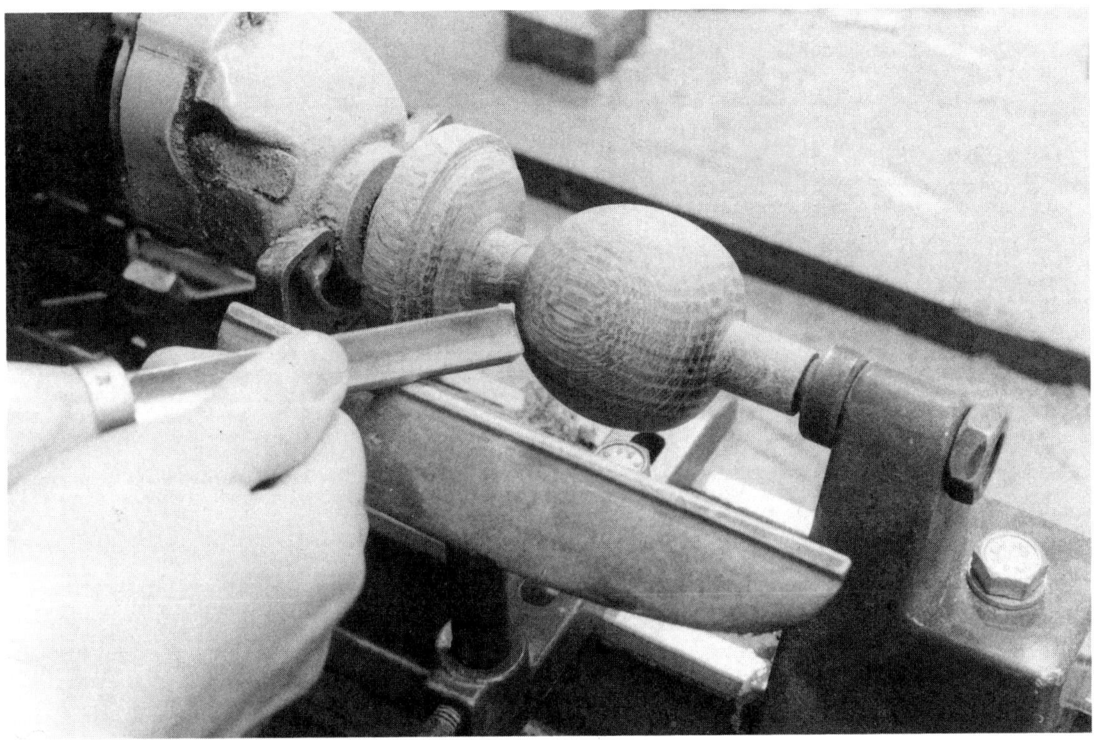

The head is made by turning the block of wood in the lathe and fashioning it to a suitable round shape with the spindle gouge. Note the projecting neck.

THE HEAD

The head is prepared from a block of wood measuring 80×60×60mm (3⅛×2⅜×2⅜in). As with the body, the centres of the two ends are marked in, and the edges and corners of the block given a preliminary rounding off with the chisel and the spokeshave before installing on the lathe.

This time, the aim of the wood-turning is to produce a round head measuring 55mm (2⅛in) in diameter, with a neck of 16mm (⅝in) diameter protruding beneath. Most of the roughing out can be done with the spindle gouge, but a parting tool will be needed to shape the neck, and a similar piece of cylindrical shaping will have to be left at the top of the head to keep the wood attached to the lathe and maintain balance as it spins. This will be removed afterwards.

It is hard to turn a perfect circle and, in any case, the head should not be absolutely spherical – in fact, you can make whatever shape you wish. When you are satisfied with the result of the turning, lay the spindle gouge and the parting tool to one side and apply a medium-grade sandpaper to the spinning head to remove any small irregularities, changing to fine-grade paper to produce a perfectly smooth finish. Always take great care when holding sandpaper against a fast-moving workpiece, wearing a thick glove to protect the fingers from burning, as the sandpaper gets very hot.

Remove the head from the lathe. Saw off the unwanted wood projecting from the top of the head and trim the neck to a length of 13 mm (½in).

Clamp the head in the vice, taking care not to compress it too hard, and drill out the 6mm (¼in)-diameter hole for the nose, placing the tip of the auger bit in an appropriate position and boring to a depth of 9mm (⅜in). The nose only sticks out a short distance so cut a piece of 6mm (¼in)-diameter dowelling to a length of about 14mm (9/16in) and round off one end with sandpaper. Mix a small amount of wood glue, apply it to the inside of the hole and press the dowel in place.

THE ARMS AND HANDS

The arms come next. These are cut from 9mm (⅜in)-diameter dowelling and consist of two upper arms and two lower arms, each of which is cut to a length of 45mm (1¾in). The hands are fashioned from small blocks of 25×13mm (1×1½in) ramin, which have firstly been drilled with a 9mm (⅜in)-diameter hole at one end to a depth of 6mm (¼in), thus permitting them to be fitted to the end of each lower arm. Also, a very small hole is drilled through the back of both hands to receive the control-strings.

Each hand is mitten-shaped, with a

The hand shapes are marked on to two pieces of wood, and cut out with the coping saw.

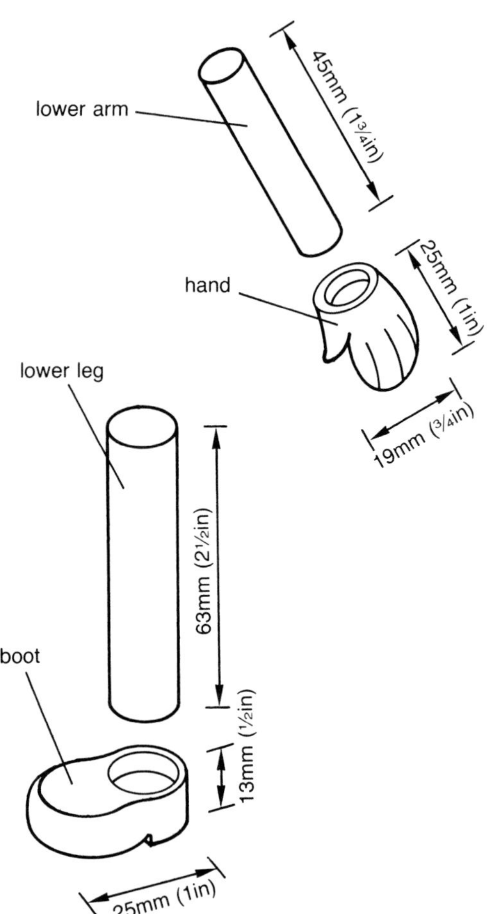

Exploded hand and foot assemblies.

small projecting thumb, and grooves are cut with a sharp marking knife to delineate the individual fingers.

THE LEGS AND FEET

The legs are similarly prepared, except that they are made from 13mm (½in)-diameter dowelling, and each of the upper and lower legs are cut to a length of 63mm (2½in). The boots that fit on the ends of the two lower legs are made from 25×13mm (1×½in) ramin blocks, measuring 25mm (1in) long, with a 13mm-diameter hole drilled in the upperside to a depth of 5mm (7/32in), the boots rounded off at the front and heels cut on the underside.

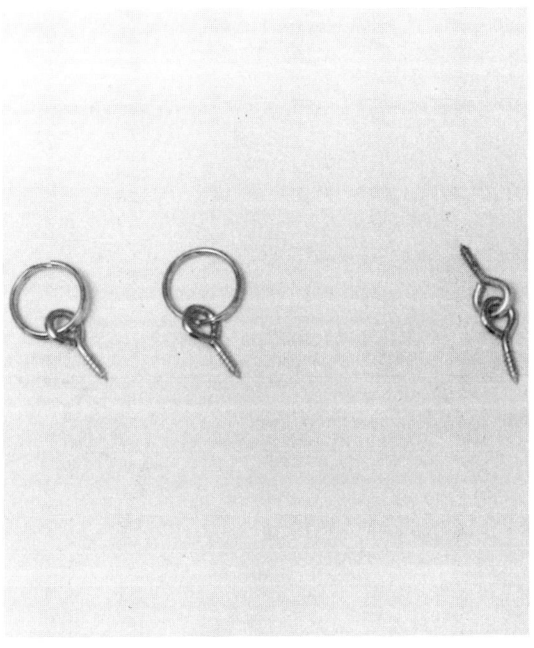

The joints are made by linking two screw-eyes together – the sort used for hanging picture frames.

ASSEMBLY

Mix more wood glue and assemble the hands to the ends of the lower arms and the boots to the ends of the lower legs, setting them to one side while the glue dries and hardens thoroughly.

The next step is to assemble the head and the limbs to the body so that it is properly articulated. Take the arms and legs first. These are jointed with small metal screw-eyes. The best source of supply for these screw-eyes is from the rings that are used to attach cord to the back of picture frames. When you buy them the rings are already fastened to the screw-eyes, but you can open the eyes out a little with a screwdriver to remove the ring. Simply interlock two screw-eyes with each other, and close them back up with a pair of pliers.

Make a pilot hole with a miniature drill-bit and bore a tiny hole wherever a screw-eye needs to be attached: at the shoulders, each end of the upper arm, the elbow end of the lower arm, at the hips, each end of the upper leg and the knee end of the lower leg. Screw each pair of coupled eyes into their pilot holes and the puppet gradually takes on a recognisable shape.

Cut the dowel block that anchors the head to the body. The dowelling is of 19mm (¾in) diameter, and it must be 16mm (⅝in) in length, so that when it is inserted down into the 25mm (1in)-deep receiver hole, there is a gap of 9mm (⅜in) above, in which the screw-eyes are concealed.

Make a pilot hole in the end of the neck and in one end of the dowel block, and fix the head to the block with a pair of coupled screw-eyes. Then mix a small quantity of wood glue, apply it to the

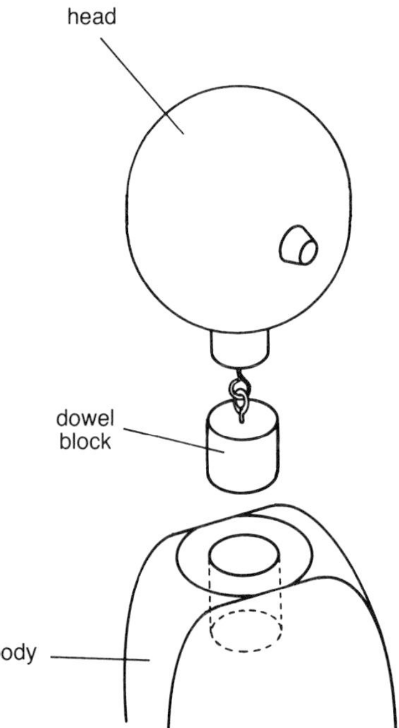

Exploded head assembly.

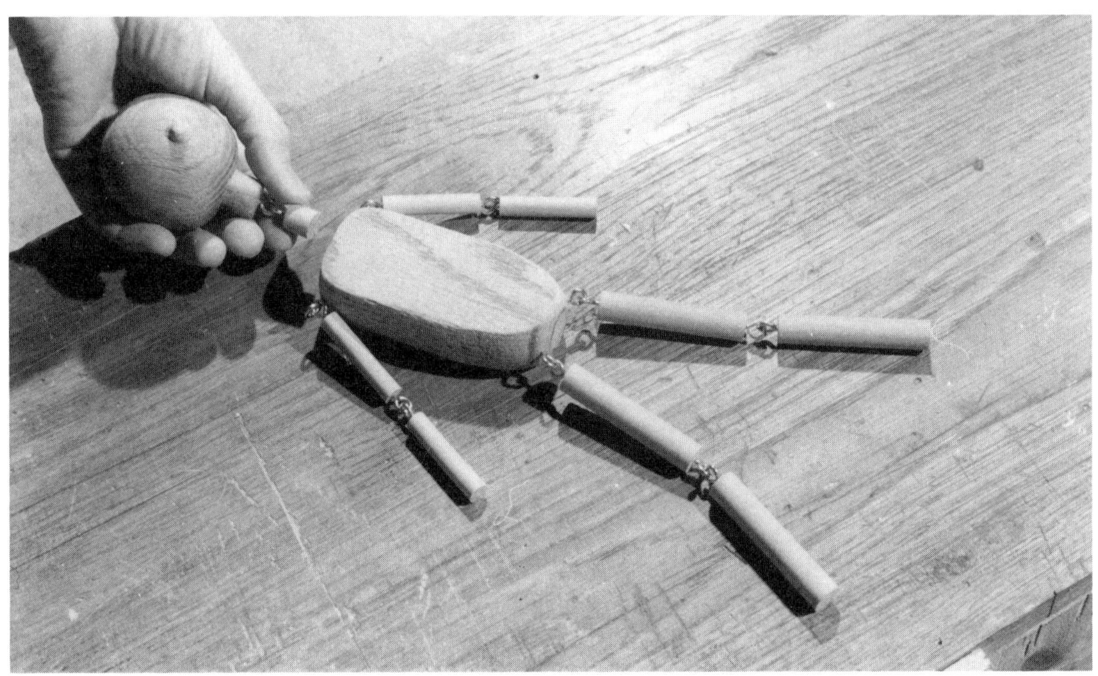

Assembling head to body.

hole drilled between the shoulders and to the block, and carefully fit the block in position, making sure that the head is directed towards the front – the nose will tell you this.

Paint the entire puppet with primer and undercoat and then apply white gloss to the head and the hands and black gloss to the boots.

THE CONTROL STRINGS

The control strings are supported on an H-shaped frame which is made from beech measuring 16×16mm (5/8×5/8in) in cross-section. The frame itself has three bars, consisting of a single long bar measuring 150mm (5⅞in) in length, to which a pair of crossbars is attached,

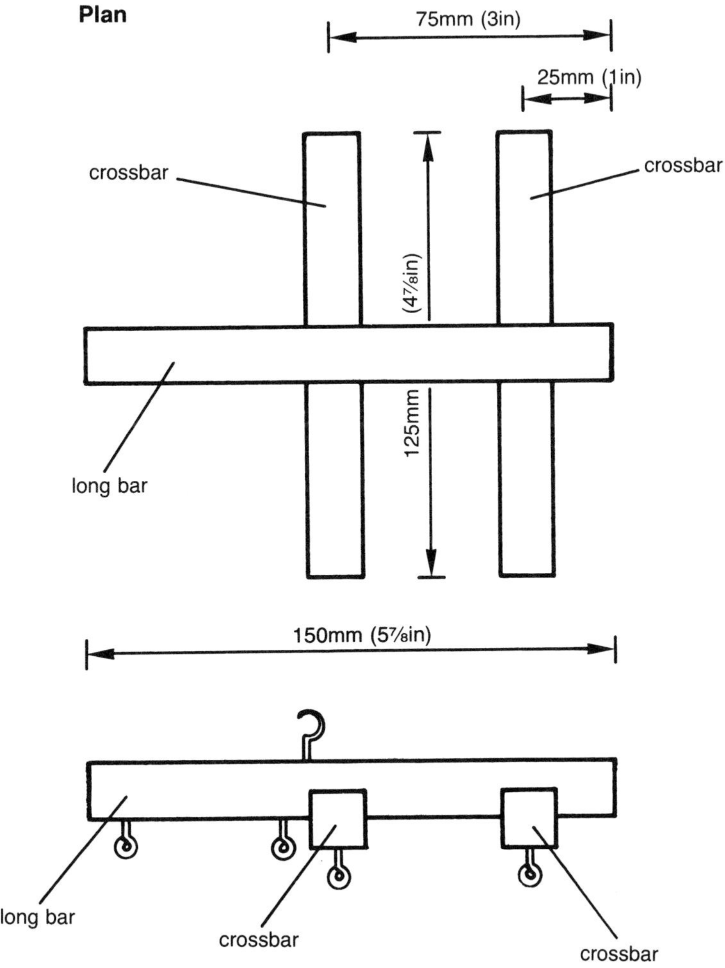

Main dimensions of the control string frame.

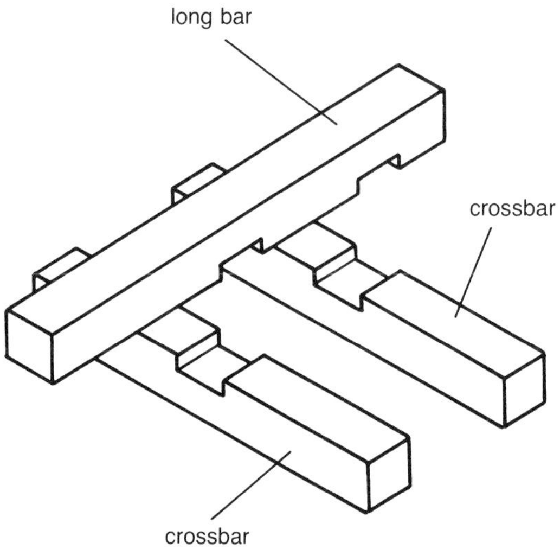

Exploded view of control string frame.

each crossbar measuring 125mm (4⅞in) in length.

The two crossbars are lap-jointed to the single long bar, each lap being cut to a depth of 4mm (3/16in) – this method is preferable to half-jointing, although it is, of course, similar in principle. The crossbars are set at a distance of 25mm (1in) and 75mm (3in) from the front end of the single support bar. Prepare the lap joints and assemble the crossbars with wood glue.

Attach six small screw-eyes to the underside of the string support frame, two on the outer ends of the front crossbar to control the hands, two on an intermediate position on the rear crossbar to control the legs, one on the long bar, slightly further back from the rear cross-

Preparing the lapped joints in the long bar and two crossbars of the string support frame.

Measure and mark in the positions of the screw-eyes in the underside of the string support frame, make small pilot holes with a panel pin, and screw home the eyes.

bar to hold the head up straight and one near the back end of the long bar to attach to the puppet's back. Finally, fix a small hook to the topside of the long bar as a means of hanging up the puppet when it is not in use.

A small screw-eye will also have to be fixed into the top of the puppet's head and the middle of its back before it is dressed in its costume, which should be made of silk material with red pom-poms. The eyes are cut from black felt and the mouth from red felt and these are stuck on to the head with adhesive.

The control strings are lengths of black thread, and their attachment points on the puppet are: for head control, to the screw-eye mounted on top of the puppet's head; for body control, to the screw-eye fixed into the back; for hand and arm control, the thread is passed through the hole drilled in each hand and tied in a knot on the palm of the hand, and for leg control, the thread is tied to the coupled screw-eyes forming the knee joint.

In all but the hand control strings, the threads will have to be passed through the costume using a sewing-needle. The distance between the string-control frame and the puppet will depend on the age and height of the child for whom the puppet is intended. Start by tying the head control string to its screw-eye on the H-frame and then, with the puppet hanging upright, tie off the remaining strings, giving it the desired posture.

The puppet can now be brought to life.

Cutting List

Body: one of 105×55×28mm (4⅛×2⅛×1⅛in)
Head: one of 80×60×60mm (3⅛×2⅜×2⅜in)
Upper arm: two of 45×9mm (1¾×⅜in) diameter
Lower arm: two of 45×9mm (1¾×⅜in) diameter
Upper leg: two of 63×13mm (2½×½in) diameter
Lower leg: two of 63×13mm (2½×½in) diameter
Hand: two of 19×25×13mm (¾×1×½in)
Boot: two of 25×25×13mm (1×1×½in)
Long bar: one of 150×16×16mm (5⅞×⅝×⅝in)
Crossbar: two of 125×16×16mm (4⅞×⅝×⅝in)

CHAPTER SEVEN

THE VINTAGE STEAM LORRY

Steam-driven commercial vehicles were once a common sight on our roads, and they were usually of characteristic appearance, with spoked wheels, solid tyres and, of course, a boiler and funnel.

The driver's cab usually had a rounded front and the livery was typical of the period.

As the lorry will be painted, the choice of wood is not particularly important, except that it should be made from hardwood. Most of the sections are fairly small, so there should be plenty of scope for dipping into the contents of your waste bin. The illustrated example was constructed from oak.

Mark out the base on a piece of 13mm (½in)-thick material, approximately 460mm (18⅛in) long and 180mm (7¹⁄₁₆in) wide. Draw a semi-circle at the front end

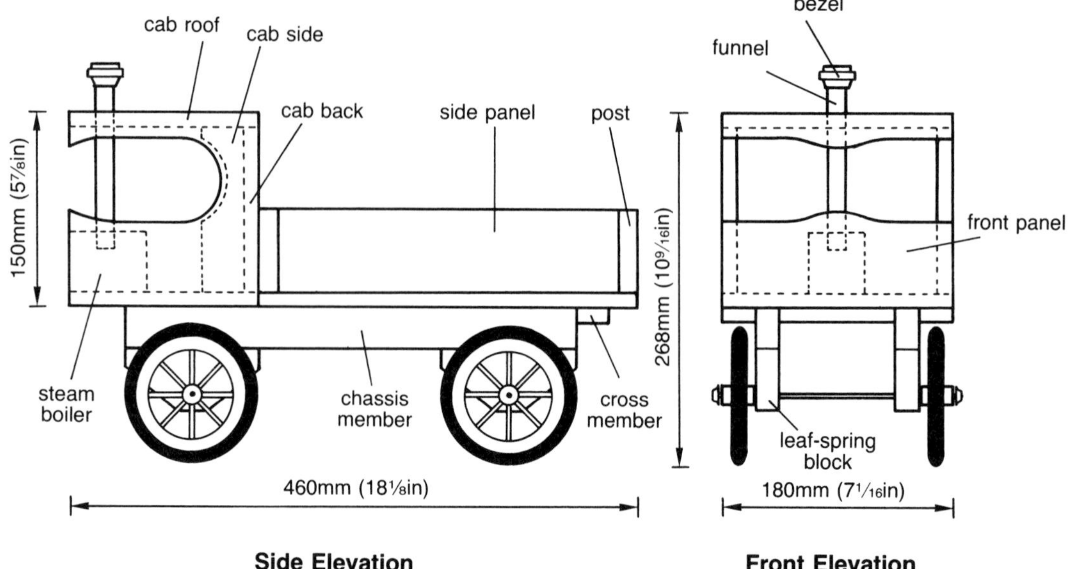

Main dimensions of the steam lorry.

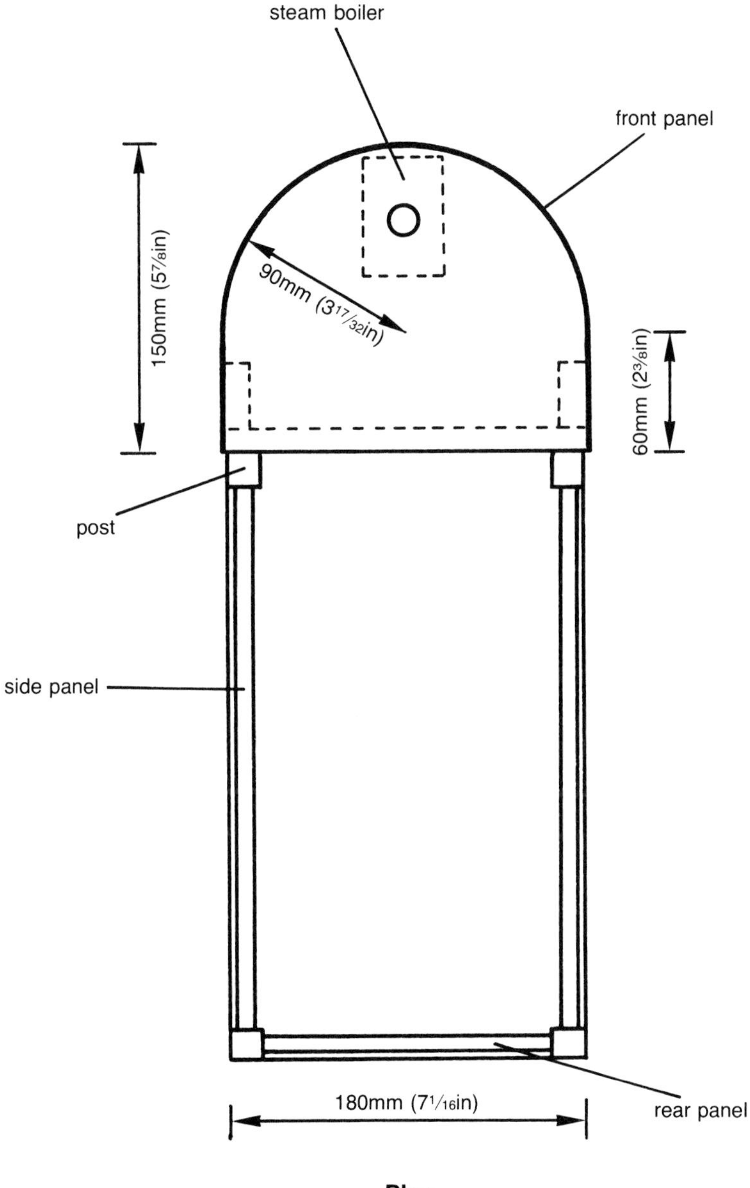

Main dimensions of the steam lorry.

measuring 90mm (3½in) in radius, and mark out a similar arrangement on a second piece of material, measuring 150mm (5⅞in) long and 13mm (½in) thick, which forms the roof of the cab.

Cut out both pieces with the electric jig-saw or handheld coping saw, clamping each piece of wood securely to the

Cut out the curved front end in the base panel with the jig-saw.

side of the workbench. Then plane down the straight edges of the base and the cab roof until they are smooth.

Cut out a 180×125mm (7 1/16×4 7/8in) panel for the back of the cab and two pieces each measuring 38mm (1½in) long by 125mm (4 7/8in) wide for the sides. You will see that these both have a curved portion removed to coincide with the curvature cut on the rounded panel that forms the front of the cab. This is cut from 2mm (3/32in)-thick plywood and measures 406×150mm (16×5 7/8in).

The marking and cutting of the plywood must be carried out with great care. The actual size of the window opening is a somewhat arbitrary amount, but you may be guided by the fact that the cab roof and the boiler have to be taken into consideration, neither of which should appear visible in the assembled lorry, and that you will not be able to cut too deeply into the cab sides without running the risk of splitting the wood.

The best way to proceed is by making a template from thin card, as this will enable you to make a rough assembly of the cab and judge the resulting appearance before cutting the plywood. The marking out of the window opening should be done with a ruler, pencil and a pair of compasses.

When you are satisfied that the card template is correct, transfer the pattern of the window opening on to the rectangular piece of plywood, and carefully cut out the unwanted portion with a sharp knife. This is quite a slow, painstaking process because, although the plywood material is only 2mm (3/32in) thick, it is fairly tough and the knife blade will have to be pressed down hard on the marked line and inched along bit by bit, particularly on the curved sections.

Eventually, the knife blade will pierce through the opposite side of the plywood, and you can then turn it over and repeat the cutting until the waste simply drops out, leaving a cleanly-cut edge that should only need a little sanding down with a fine-grade sandpaper.

As the semi-circular curves at either end of the window must correspond with curved portions removed from the two cab sides, it is wiser to complete the preparation of the cab front before marking and cutting the sides, once again using the card template for the purpose.

Cut the block of wood for the boiler and a length of 16mm (5/8in)-diameter dowelling for the funnel. Although the cab has a rounded front, it is not strictly necessary to round off the front end of the boiler, because it is hardly visible. All you need do is position it on the base so

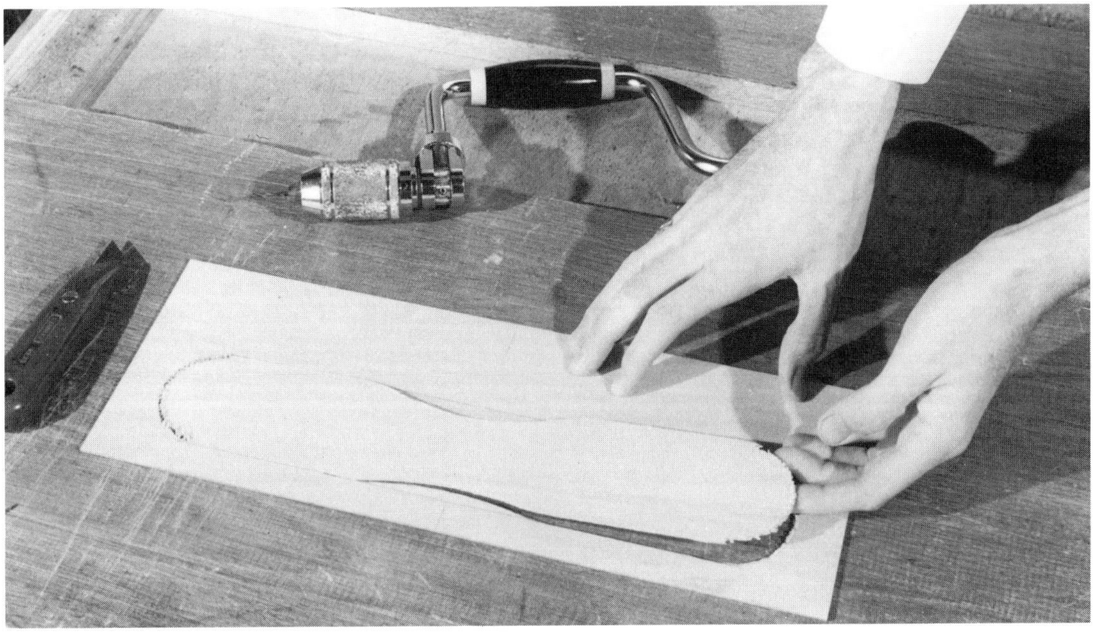

Cut out the cab window opening in the plywood panel using a sharp knife and plenty of patience.

that its two front corners just touch the curved front of the base. If the receiver hole for the funnel is marked in a dead-centre position on the top surface of the boiler, this position can also be marked on the roof panel.

Drill a 16mm (⅝in)-diameter hole through the roof panel using a centre-bit mounted in a handbrace. To prevent the underside of the panel from splitting as the drill-bit breaks through, stop drilling at the moment that the pointed tip emerges on the opposite side, then turn the piece over and complete the drilling.

Mount the block for the boiler in the vice and drill down in the marked position to a depth of approximately 13mm (½in).

Set the boiler and funnel to one side for the moment and assemble the cab roof, the back and the two sides to the base with dowel joints, marking in the dowel position accurately so that the curvature of the front of the roof lines up exactly with that of the base. Drill the dowel holes with a 6mm (¼in)-diameter auger bit and cut the dowels from matching 6mm (¼in)-diameter material. As a guide to the depth of the holes, those bored down into the surfaces of the base and the roof should be no greater than 9mm (⅜in), whereas those bored into the edges of the sides and the back panel are less restricted and may be up to 13mm (½in) deep, giving an overall dowel length of 19mm (¾in).

Mix a small quantity of wood glue, apply this to the dowels and their holes and, for added strength, brush glue onto all abutting surfaces, tapping them together gently with the mallet. At the same time, fit the cross-member to the

Assemble the cab sides to the back panel and the base, before adding the roof. All the joints are dowelled and glued.

The plywood front panel must be thoroughly soaked in water to make it flexible enough to bend around the curved front. G-clamps and blocks of scrap wood hold it in position while the glue sets.

The Pencil Dice (Chapter 1).

The Table-Top Skittles (Chapter 2).

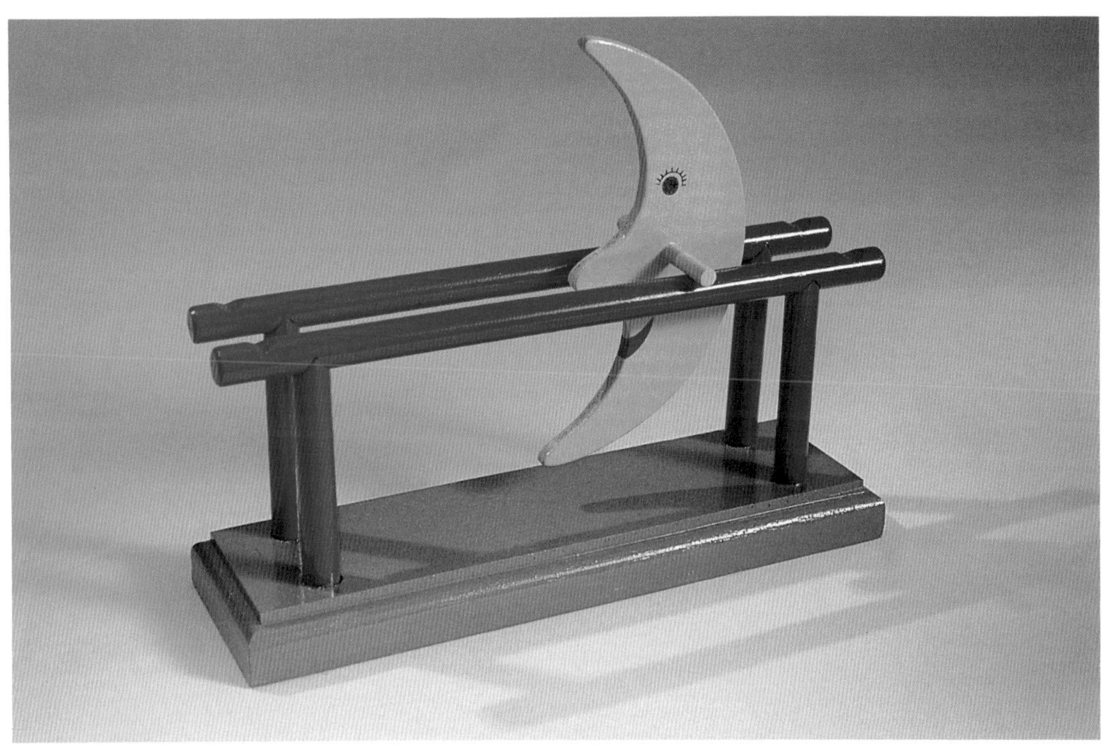

The Acrobatic Moon (Chapter 3).

The Clock Puzzle (Chapter 4).

The Pull-Along Duck (Chapter 5).

The Vintage Steam Lorry (Chapter 7).

The String Puppet (Chapter 6).

The Garden Table and Chair Set (Chapter 8).

The Doll's Chest of Drawers (Chapter 9).

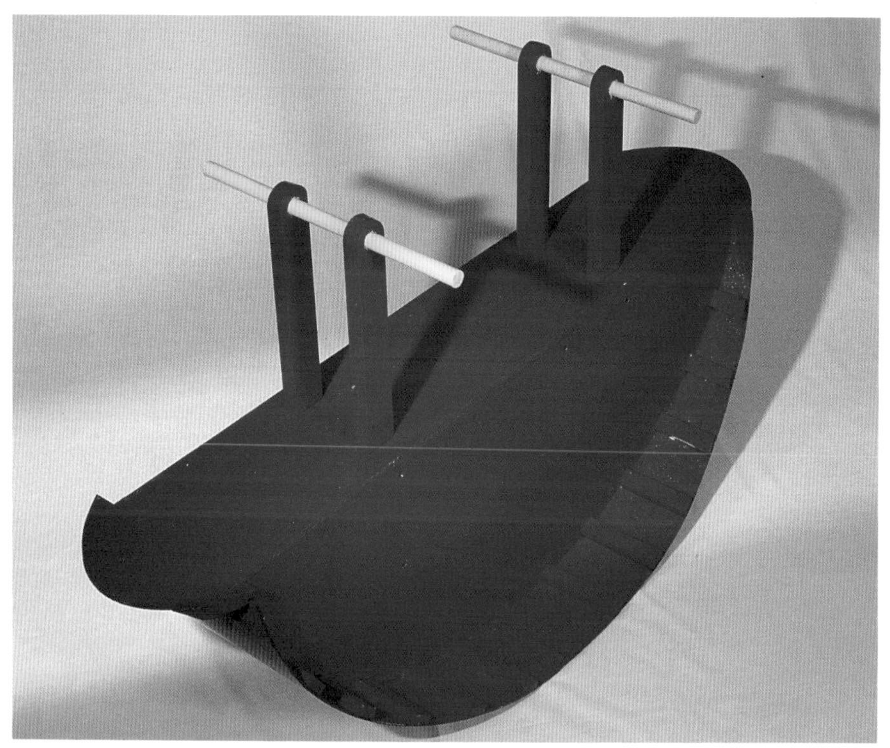

The Oval Rocker (Chapter 10).

The Castle Toy Box (Chapter 11).

The Farm Tractor and Cart (Chapter 12).

The Toboggan (Chapter 13).

The Windmill Money Box (Chapter 14).

The Horse Tricycle (Chapter 15).

underside of the base close to the rear end. This is also attached with dowel joints and gives strength to the base.

When all the cab joints have set hard, fit the plywood in place. As this has to wrap around the front of the cab, you should first soak the plywood in warm water to soften the wood, thus making it easier to bend without snapping. Let it soak for an hour and gently work it into a curve, applying progressively greater hand pressure.

Once it bends sufficiently to follow the contour of the cab, clamp it to the sides with a length of clean scrap wood and a G-clamp at each side. This will hold it firmly in the required position while the plywood dries in readiness for gluing.

After several hours, remove the clamps and you will find that the plywood remains curved, although it will still have an inclination to straighten out. Apply a fresh mixture of wood glue around the edges of the cab and to the inside surface of the plywood, re-clamping it in place for at least a day. The joint should be strengthened at each end by tapping in a row of veneer pins.

Cut the two chassis members from 32×16mm (1¼×⅝in) material, mounting them with dowel joints to the underside of the base from the cross-member forward, so that they lie parallel with the sides and are set in by 25mm (1in) from the edges. Glue them in position.

Next, cut the four leaf-spring blocks

The positions of the leaf-spring blocks must be set very accurately on the underside of the chassis members, to ensure that the lorry runs in a straight line. The blocks are dowel-jointed in position.

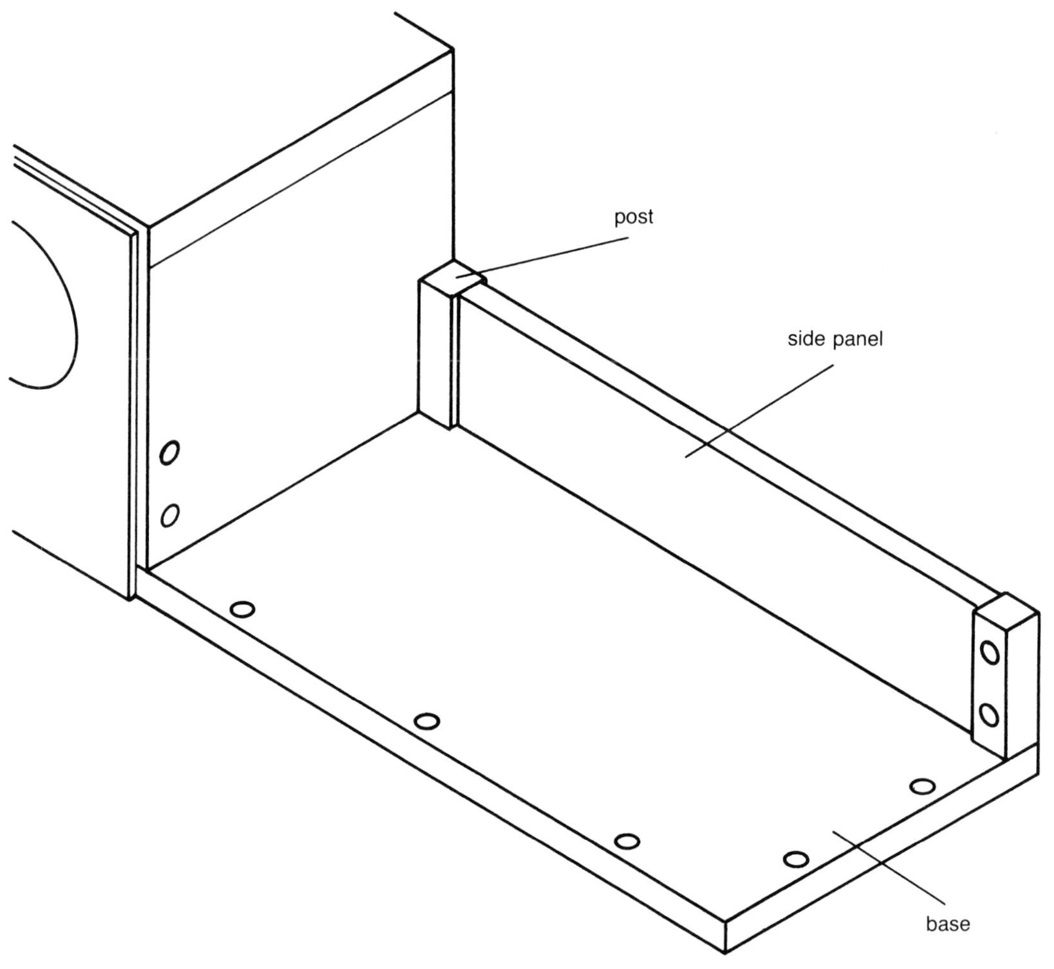

Partial assembly of posts, side panels and rear panel – dowel hole positions shown.

from rectangular pieces of material each measuring 100×48mm (4×1⅞in) and 16mm (⅝in) in thickness to match that of the chassis members. Drill a 6mm (¼in)-diameter hole near the bottom of each block to receive the wheel axles – all four holes should be in exactly the same position.

The blocks are assembled to the chassis members in such a way that they lie flush with the extremities of the two long pieces. They are dowel-jointed and glued in place with two dowels per leaf-spring block, each one set in by 25mm (1in) from the end.

The load-carrying platform behind the cab of the lorry is fitted with an imitation drop-side arrangement, in which the two side panels and single rear panel are dowel-jointed to the square-section upright posts, the entire structure being dowel-jointed to the upper surface of the base and the rear surface of the cab back.

The four upright posts each measure 60mm (2⅜in) long and are cut from 16×16mm (⅝×⅝in) material, whereas the two side panels are cut from 13mm (½in)-thick hardwood measuring 280×60mm (11×2⅜in), and the rear panel from wood of the same thickness measuring 148×60mm (5 13/16×2⅜in).

The number of dowels and their exact positioning is not critical. Try using two dowels between each panel and upright, three dowels spaced at regular intervals along the bottom edge of each side panel, two along the bottom edge of the rear panel and one dowel each to join the two posts to the cab back. Glue all the joints and assemble the three panels and four posts simultaneously.

Glue the boiler block to the floor of the cab and attach the funnel, which is cut from a length of 16mm (⅝in)-diameter dowelling that projects 25mm (1in) above the cab roof. Glue the funnel into the boiler block. As a finishing touch, the top of the funnel is capped with a flange. This is turned on the lathe from a piece of 32mm (1¼in)-diameter dowelling. This is probably the hardest part of the project and, if you do not have access to a lathe, or lathe accessory powered by an electric drill, the flange may be omitted.

To make the flange, take a length of 32mm (1¼in) dowelling measuring at least 75mm (3in), and cut both the ends perfectly square. Measure and mark the centre at each end, making a small pilot hole with the bradawl.

Before turning the flange, a 16mm (⅝in)-diameter hole must be drilled into

The two side panels and one rear panel are assembled, together with the two upright posts, on to the base and the cab back panel.

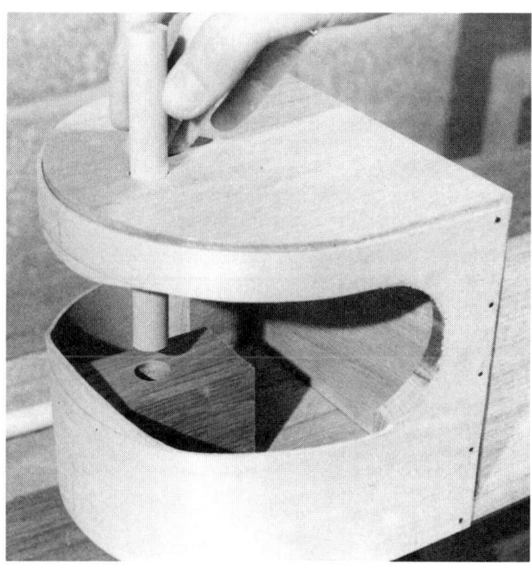

The funnel is passed through the hole in the cab roof, and glued into the receiver hole drilled in the steam boiler.

it to receive the funnel, since this cannot possibly be done afterwards. The only problem is that once the hole has been drilled into it, the dowelling cannot be mounted on the lathe.

To overcome this, drill the hole to a depth of 38mm (1½in), pencilling in a corresponding line around the circumference of the dowel at this point. Now mark two more lines around the circumference 8mm (5⁄16in) to either side of this first line to delineate the extremities of the flange.

Take a piece of 16mm (⅝in)-diameter dowelling and mark off 25mm (1in) from one end in pencil, then mix a small amount of wood glue, apply some to the end of the dowelling and insert it into the hole drilled in the larger dowel as far as the 25mm (1in) mark. Place to one side

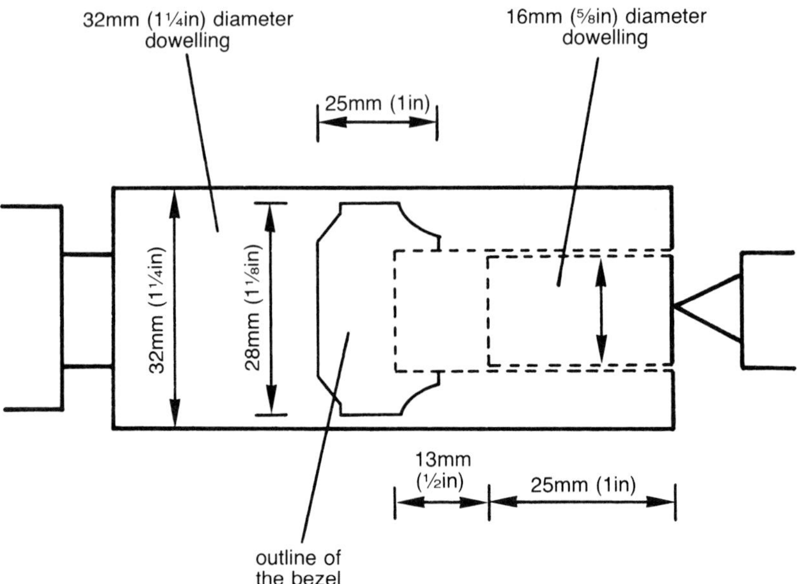

Dowel mounted in the lathe ready for turning the bezel for the funnel.

for a day so that the glue can dry and set hard.

Cut off the projecting piece of 16mm ($\frac{5}{8}$in)-diameter dowelling so that the end of the 32mm ($1\frac{1}{4}$in)-diameter piece is once again perfectly flush, but this time with the smaller diameter dowel glued inside to a depth of 25mm (1in), leaving a 13mm ($\frac{1}{2}$in)-long cavity. Re-establish the centre of this end and mark with the bradawl.

Carefully mount the dowel in the lathe ready for turning. Using appropriate wood-turning tools, work the flange shape between the two outermost pencil lines, reducing the diameter and creating the two tapers either end. Make sure that you do not reduce the diameter too much, otherwise you will cut into the cavity and ruin the work. Finally, remove the turning from the lathe and trim off the ends with the hacksaw. Apply some wood glue to the hole in the flange, and tap it gently on to the end of the funnel.

The lorry is now ready for painting. Although you will probably want to choose your own livery and colour scheme, the underside, the chassis members and leaf-spring blocks should be painted black. Use a paint that is safe and non-toxic.

The last step is to fit the wheels and axles. The wheels are 100mm (4in) in diameter, having white spoked centres with black rubber tyres, and a 6mm ($\frac{1}{4}$in)-diameter axle hole to receive the steel axle. The wheels, axle material and spring hub caps can be obtained from model shops.

Allowing for the thickness of the wheel centres, add an extra 6mm ($\frac{1}{4}$in) per wheel for the spring hub caps and cut two axles to length with the hacksaw. Push them through the holes in the leaf-spring blocks, fit the wheels in position and secure them with the spring hub caps, which are tapped gently in place with the mallet.

The lorry is now ready to set off on its first journey.

Cutting List

Base: one of 460×180×13mm ($18\frac{1}{8}$×$7\frac{1}{16}$×$\frac{1}{2}$in)
Cab roof: one of 150×180×13mm ($5\frac{7}{8}$×$7\frac{1}{16}$×$\frac{1}{2}$in)
Cab back: one of 180×125×13mm ($7\frac{1}{16}$×$4\frac{7}{8}$×$\frac{1}{2}$in)
Cab side: two of 38×125×13mm ($1\frac{1}{2}$×$4\frac{7}{8}$× ×$\frac{1}{2}$in)
Front panel: one of 406×150×2mm (16×$5\frac{7}{8}$×$\frac{3}{32}$in)
Cross-member: two of 180×25×13mm ($7\frac{1}{16}$×1×$\frac{1}{2}$in)
Chassis member: two of 360×32×16mm ($14\frac{1}{8}$×$1\frac{1}{4}$×$\frac{5}{8}$in)
Leaf-spring block: four of 100×48×16mm (4×$1\frac{7}{8}$×$\frac{5}{8}$in)
Upright post: four of 60×16×16mm ($2\frac{3}{8}$×$\frac{5}{8}$×$\frac{5}{8}$)
Side panel: two of 280×60×13mm (11×$2\frac{3}{8}$×$\frac{1}{2}$in)
Rear panel: one of 148×60×13mm ($5\frac{13}{16}$×$2\frac{3}{8}$×$\frac{1}{2}$in)
Steam boiler: one of 75×50×45mm (3×2×$1\frac{3}{4}$in)
Funnel: one of 140×16mm ($5\frac{1}{2}$×$\frac{5}{8}$in) diameter
Flange: one of 25×32mm (1×$1\frac{1}{4}$in) diameter

Chapter Eight

The Garden Table and Chair Set

The garden is often one of a child's main sources of interest and adventure, and a miniature table and chair set is ideal for entertaining a favourite teddy-bear or doll.

The designs for these two pieces of outdoor furniture are kept as simple as possible. There is always a slight problem when scaling down from an accepted standard size, because the question arises as to how small the table and chair should be. The dimensions depend on the age and size of the child, but for guidance, the illustrated set will suit a boy or girl aged between two and four years.

The material used to make the table and chair is ramin, which is a light-coloured and straight-grained hardwood. Various standard sizes are sold in DIY shops, usually in lengths ranging from 6ft to 8ft (1,830mm to 2,440mm).

THE CHAIR

Taking the chair first, the front legs are cut to length from 25×25mm (1×1in) ramin, and the back legs are marked out on a piece of 50×25mm (2×1in) material, noting that there is a rearward rake to the top and the bottom of each leg from the point where the side seat rail is attached. In both cases, the rake extends for 25mm (1in), and the legs are shaped in such a way that they are marked to a width of 25mm (1in) from the seat rail level down to the ground, tapering up to a width of 19mm (¾in) at the top.

Mark both sides of each leg identically in pencil, so that these lines can be followed for the cutting out of the waste.

There are various ways of removing the sloped areas of waste. The wood may be clamped in the workbench vice and the waste cut away with the coping saw; or clamped securely to the edge of the workbench and removed with the jig-saw. Either way, work the saw blade closely to the pencilled line just on the waste side. The use of either tool will require great care to ensure that the blade does not stray off course on one side or other. Once the sawing is complete, the small amount of remaining waste is removed with the spokeshave, and the edges rubbed down with medium-grade sandpaper.

There is an alternative method of removing the waste from the rear legs, and that is to plane off all the unwanted wood down to the marked lines. For

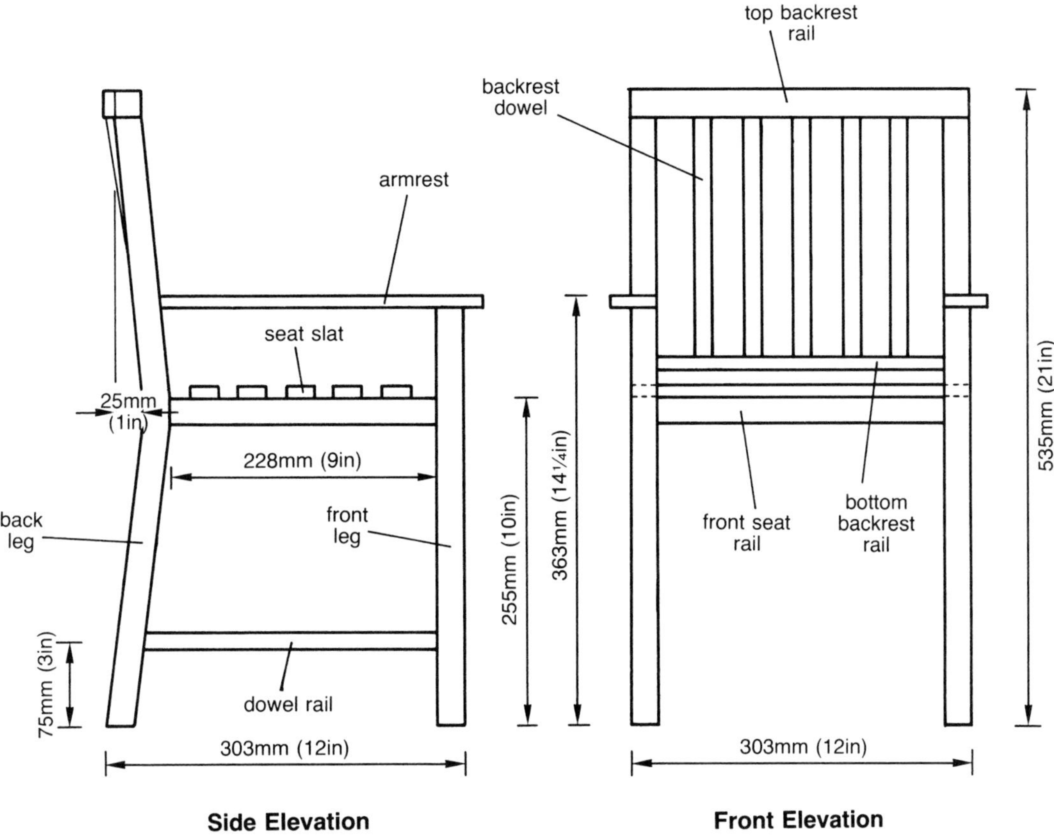

Main dimensions of garden chair.

obvious reasons it is impossible to manipulate a smoothing plane on an inside concave curve so, in this instance, the spokeshave will have to be employed. If that fails you can saw a series of cuts down to within 2mm (3⁄32in) of the pencil line and chop away the waste with a chisel and mallet. A wide-bladed chisel should be used, preferably 19mm (¾in) or 25mm (1in) wide. The final bit of waste can be removed by scraping with the chisel and then rubbing down with sandpaper.

The front, back and side seat rails are all cut from 25×13mm (1×½in) ramin, their ends marked square and sawn to length with the tenon saw. They are each assembled to the legs with dowel joints using two 6mm-diameter dowels per joint. The rail positions are first marked on two adjacent surfaces of each leg, taking care that they are all at exactly the same height from the ground. For this, the rakes of the rear legs must be taken into account.

Square in the positions of the joints, which are all 25mm long, equal to the width of the rails. Set the fence of the marking gauge so that the spur scribes a line halfway across the 25mm width and

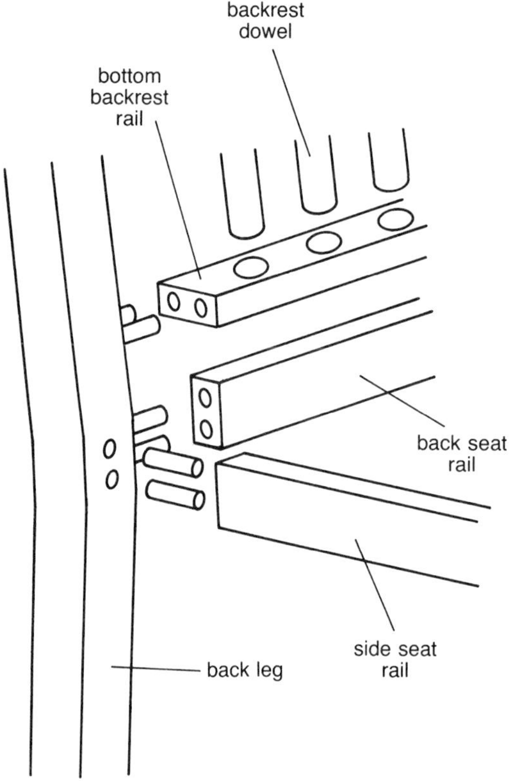

Exploded dowel joints for the chair.

thickness of the front and rear legs; then adjust the fence so that a line can be inscribed along the end-grain of the rails, midway across the thickness.

Set in the dowel hole positions by 6mm (¼in) from each end of the rails, and similarly for the lines scribed on the legs, so that they correspond. Mark the positions with the point of a bradawl and drill out the holes using a 6mm (¼in)-diameter auger bit mounted in the hand-brace.

For the legs, clamp the piece securely to the side of the workbench, or hold it firmly in the vice, and drill each hole to a depth of 9mm (⅜in). Try to avoid drilling any deeper, otherwise each pair of holes would meet up with the pair drilled in the adjacent surface and, although this would not matter greatly, it would be better to avoid it.

For the rails, clamp the material upright in the vice and drill to a depth of 19mm (¾in) into the end-grain. This depth is not so critical, but there is little benefit to be gained from boring any deeper.

Measure and cut the dowels to size that will be used to fit these holes. Eight 6mm (¼in)-diameter dowels will be required, each one being 25mm (1in) in length, slightly less than the combined depth of the holes bored in the rails and legs. The ends of each dowel are chamfered by giving a few twists in a pencil sharpener to make for an easier entry into the hole. And, on that subject, a word of warning: because some drill-bits are made to imperial measurements and dowelling cut to metric diameters, or vice versa, there may be a marginal difference between what amounts to ¼in and 6mm. If the dowel is slightly bigger than the hole, there will be a strain on the rail which is, after all, only 13mm (½in) thick, and the wood will split.

Make a trial fitting with a piece of scrap 25×13mm (1×½in) ramin and a length of 6mm-diameter dowelling, to see if the dowel goes easily into the hole. If it does not, reduce its diameter a little by paring down around the circumference with a narrow chisel, until it fits without needing any great pressure. Do the same for all the dowels.

In addition to the side seat rails, the front and back legs are also joined near the bottom by a length of 16mm (⅝in)-diameter dowelling, which serves to strengthen each of the side assemblies, and thus cope with the inevitable tilting

Fit together one of the side assemblies, applying glue to the dowels and the dowel holes and tapping the front and rear legs to the side seat rail and dowel rail.

back of the chair when it is in use – a practice to be discouraged.

The two dowel rails are set 75mm (3in) up from the bottom of the front and back legs, and mounted midway across the thickness of the pieces. Allowing for the rake of the back legs, drill out receiver holes for the dowelling to a depth of 9mm (3/8in) in all four legs. Measure and cut two pieces of dowelling to length from 16mm (5/8in)-diameter material.

Mix a small quantity of waterproof wood glue and apply it with a small brush to the dowel pegs and their receiver holes for the side rails to the front and back legs, and for the 16mm (5/8in)-diameter dowels and their holes. Tap the two side assemblies together with the mallet. They should, of course, be identical when placed side by side, and this is a good opportunity to make a comparison to see that they are equal.

When both side assemblies have dried thoroughly, prepare to join them together with the front and back seat rails. But, before proceeding with this stage, note that the backrest must also be constructed from a top and bottom backrest rail and five lengths of dowelling.

The bottom backrest rail is merely a duplication of the front and back seat rails, being cut to the same length from 25×13mm (1×1/2in) ramin, only that instead of being mounted vertically with respect to its width, this rail is set just off the horizontal, the small angle being accounted for by the rake.

The top backrest rail is cut from more 50×25mm (2×1in) ramin, and this extends to take in the top end-grain of both rear legs, and is given a gentle backward curve to make for a more comfortable sitting posture. Once it has been marked, shaped with the spokeshave and cut to length, the top backrest is given a single 6mm (1/4in)-diameter dowel joint into the top of each back leg.

The five backrest rails are cut from 16mm (5/8in)-diameter dowelling, and set at regular intervals in receiver holes drilled in the underside of the top backrest rail and the upper side of the bottom rail. Clearly, as the bottom rail is only 13mm (1/2in) thick, the holes can only be shallow, and should be bored to a depth of no more than 6mm (1/4in).

Cut the five dowels accurately to length and make a trial fitting to ensure that the two backrest rails align with their indicated positions – the bottom rail having its dowel-joint holes measured and cut 50mm (2in) above the back seat rail – and then mix more wood glue and assemble the front and back seat rails and the bottom backrest rail using the necessary dowel pegs, tapping the joints home.

Fit the bottom backrest rail and the front and back rails to one side assembly.

Next, apply glue to all ten receiver holes for the five backrest dowels, and to the dowel joints securing the top backrest rail to the end of the two rear legs.

Bring the whole backrest assembly together, placing the dowels in their holes before knocking the top rail down into position.

The armrests are shaped in such a way that they commence at a maximum width of 50mm (2in) at the front and taper gradually inwards to a width of 25mm (1in) at the point where they butt up against the rear leg. Measure and mark them out on a piece of 70×13mm (2¾× ½in) material. Cut them to size with the saw, plane the sloped edges, and bevel the rear end-grain slightly to match the rake of the back leg.

Mark two 6mm (¼in)-diameter dowel joints on the back leg and the end-grain of the armrest, and a single dowel joint to fix the top of the front leg to the underside of the armrest, arranging the position of the armrest in such a manner that its inner edge lies flush with the inner edge of the leg. Glue the joints together and fit the two armrests.

Arrange the five seat slats at regular intervals, mark in their positions and glue them to the upper edge of the two side seat rails.

Cut the five seat slats from 25×13mm (1×½in) material, and arrange them at regular intervals between the two side seat rails, gluing them in position. These are simply butt joints, relying on the strength of the glue to hold them in place.

Sandpaper all the corners of the chair to round them off, paying particular attention to the top of the backrest and the front ends of both armrests, where sharp corners could cause injury to the child.

THE TABLE

The matching table resembles the chair in several respects, most notably in the general method of construction and the fact that it is slatted.

In terms of size, its height is slightly greater than the distance from the ground up to the seat of the chair, the difference being no more than 38mm (1½in).

The table top is square and composed of slats mounted on a simple framework that bears a close likeness to the construction of the chair.

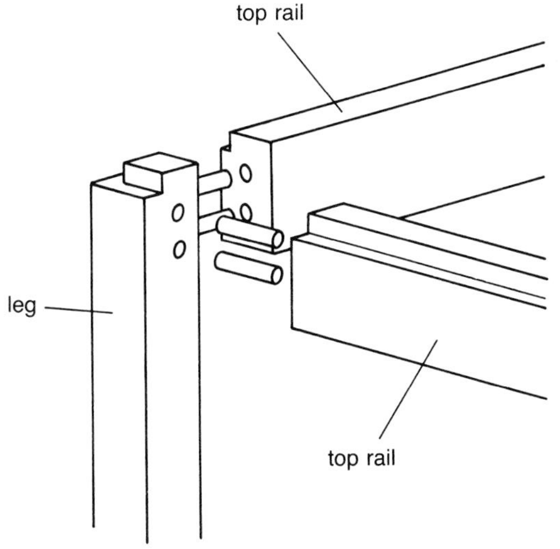

Exploded dowel joints for the table.

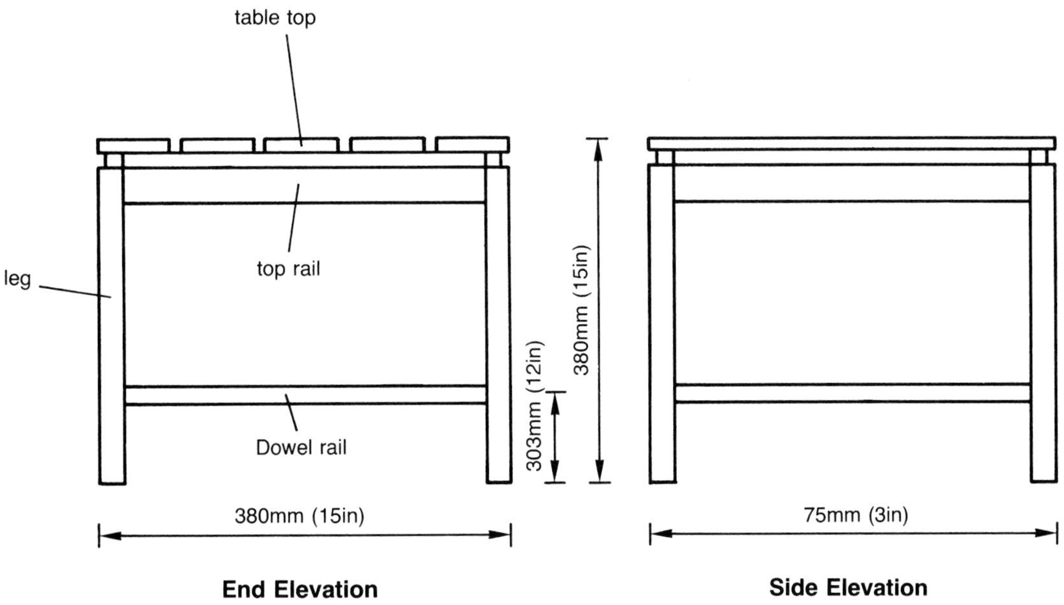

Main dimensions of garden table.

Start by cutting the four legs to length from 25×25mm (1×1in) ramin, making sure that the ends are cut perfectly square. Now cut the four identical top rails to length from 45×22mm (1¾×⅞in) material. The rails are dowel-jointed to the legs, their inner surfaces being arranged to lie flush so that, when viewed from the outside, the rails are set back by 3mm (⅛in) from the outer edges of the legs.

The dowel joints are marked in the same way as for the chair, using the marking gauge, tape measure and pencil, using two 6mm (¼in)-diameter dowels per joint, only this time they are set in by 16mm (⅝in) from the edges of the rails. With the top edge of each rail aligning with the top end of each leg, mark the corresponding dowel positions on two adjacent surfaces of all four legs, and bore out the holes with the 6mm (¼in)-diameter auger bit to a depth of 9mm (⅜in).

Strengthen the bottom of the legs with dowel rails cut from 16mm (⅝in)-diameter ramin dowelling, setting their receiver holes 75mm (3in) up from ground level, as with the chair, but, on this occasion run a dowel between each of the legs making a total of four rails instead of the chair's two.

Before assembling the top rails and dowel rails to the legs, rebate the upper outside edge along each top rail, also taking in the top of the legs. The amount to be rebated is 6mm (¼in) wide by 6mm (¼in) deep for the legs but, since the rails are set back by 3mm (⅛in) from the outer surfaces of the legs, their rebates will be 6mm (¼in) wide by 3mm (⅛in) deep.

Mark the rebates on the legs with squared pencil lines and along the rails with inscribed marking gauge lines; and remove the waste with the tenon saw and plough plane respectively. The electric router may be used as an alternative to the plough, if you have one available.

Drill a pair of dowel holes in two adjacent sides at the top of each table leg.

Cut sixteen 6mm (¼in)-diameter dowel pegs to a length of 25mm (1in) each, chamfering the ends and trimming where necessary. Mix some wood glue, apply it to each of the joints in turn and assemble the table framework. Cramp up the assembly until the glue has set hard.

When the cramps have been removed, cut the slats for the table top from the 75×13mm (3×½in) ramin, and arrange the five pieces regularly on top of the framework. Mark their positions with faint pencil lines, and assemble them with wood glue. There is no need to screw them in position or use dowels, as the glue will be strong enough to make for a lasting butt joint at each point where the underside of a slat touches the framework.

Apply glue to the dowels and dowel holes, and fit the legs to the top rails.

Arrange the five table slats at regular intervals on top of the table framework, marking their positions in pencil, and assembling with wood glue.

Rub down all the edges and corners with medium-grade sandpaper, and then switch to fine-grade paper to obtain a smooth finish, always rubbing in the same direction as the grain.

In choosing a suitable finish for the table and chair, remember that they are intended for outdoor use and could easily get wet, so a water-resisting varnish is the most appropriate. Several coats will ensure that the wood is well-protected, giving a surface that can easily be wiped clean.

Cutting List

THE CHAIR

Front leg: two of 350×25×25mm (13¾×1×1in)
Back leg: two of 510×50×25mm (20×2×1in)
Top backrest rail: one of 303×50×25mm (12×2×1in)
Bottom backrest rail: one of 253×25×13mm (10×1×½in)
Front and back seat rail: two of 253×25×13mm (10×1×½in)
Side seat rail: two of 228×25×13mm (9×1×½in)
Armrest: two of 280×70×13mm (11×2¾×½in)
Seat slat: five of 300×25×13mm (11¾×1×½in)
Backrest dowel: five of 235×16mm (9¼×⅝in) diameter
Dowel rail: two of 265×16mm (10⁷⁄₁₆×⅝in) diameter

THE TABLE

Leg: four of 290×25×25mm (11⅜×1×1in)
Top rail: four of 330×45×22mm (13×1¾×⅞in)
Table top: five of 380×70×13mm (15×2¾×½in)
Dowel rail: four of 340×16mm (13⅜×⅝in) diameter

CHAPTER NINE

THE DOLL'S CHEST OF DRAWERS

This small wooden box with its three velvet-lined compartments is really a minature chest of drawers for a doll; but when the doll's owner no longer wants to use it for that purpose, it immediately becomes a jewellery box. Only the middle and bottom drawers actually pull out; the top drawer is fixed in position, and the lid hinges upwards to reveal its contents.

As this is a toy that could easily become a valued ornament over the years, it is important to make it from good quality wood. There are several excellent hardwoods from which to make your choice, and this example is made from

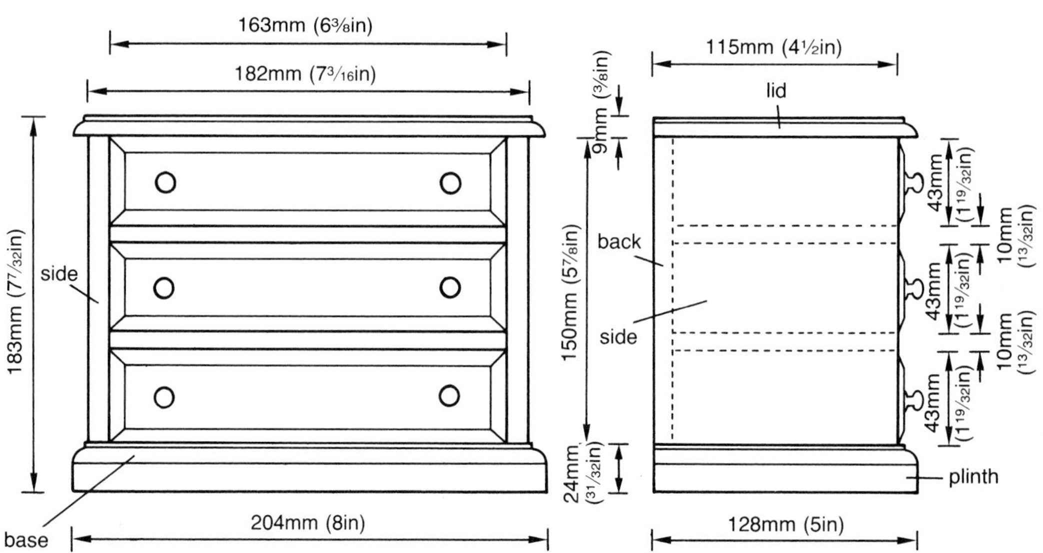

Main dimensions of the chest of drawers.

left-over sapele, which has a very finely textured grain.

Even off-cut material has to be prepared to the required finished sizes, so the first task is to pick out the best pieces of waste wood and plane them down to the two thicknesses indicated in the cutting list. If anything, leave them a little on the full side.

Choose the best 9mm (3⁄8in)-thick samples for the lid and the base and plane them to a width of 128mm (5in). Mark in the length of each piece with the square and pencil and cut them both to size with the jig-saw or tenon saw.

In each case, three of the edges are given a decorative moulding and the best tool for this job is the electric router fitted with a corner round cutter – although the plough plane will produce the same result provided that it is fitted with a special attachment that permits it to cut across the grain of the wood.

Set the router to cut to the desired depth so that it gives a good edge profile, but do not attempt to make the cut in one single go. Having set the depth of the cut, make several runs with the router, commencing with only a small cut and increasing each time until you make the final run at the required depth. This ensures that the router does not work under a heavy load, overheating the cutter, with the possible risk of scorching the wood.

Work the moulding first on the two end-grains, taking care when finishing the run that you slow down sufficiently to prevent the end of the wood splitting. Finally, cut the moulding on the front edge, working the router along the grain. For all three cuts, the material should be clamped firmly to the end of the workbench. When the edges are finished, rub

Cut the groove in the side panel with the router, so that it receives the tongue cut in the back panel.

down with fine-grade sandpaper to remove any loose strands of material and give a smooth surface.

The next step is to measure and cut the two side panels and the back panel to size. Here, there is an important distinction to be made regarding the direction of the grain. The grain for the side panels runs from top to bottom, whereas for the back panel it runs from side to side. Note that the back panel lies flush with the rear edge of the base panel, and the side panels are each set in by 3mm (1⁄8in) from the decorative edge moulding.

The three panels are fitted together with lapped joints. Grooves are cut on the rear inside faces of the side panels to accept tongues cut at each end of the back panel. The grooves are 6mm (1⁄4in) thick and set in 3mm (1⁄8in) from the rear edge; they are cut to a depth of 5mm

(7/32in) with the router equipped with a 6mm (1/4in)-diameter straight router bit. The tongue is cut similarly to a thickness of 6mm (1/4in), with a 3mm (1/8in)-thick shoulder portion and a depth of 5mm (7/32in), the waste being cut away with the tenon saw.

Fit the joints temporarily together and place the assembly on the base panel to check that they stand square. Lightly pencil in the position of the three panels.

Cut the two drawer rails and four drawer runners to size. They all share a common thickness of 10mm (13/32in), but the depth of the rails is 15mm (19/32in) compared with 6mm (1/4in) for the runners. Cut them all to length, the two rails being 164mm (6 1/2in) long and the four runners being 90mm (3 1/2in).

As each of the three drawers will be made to the same dimensions, the drawer rails and runners divide the height of the box into equal thirds. Mark in their positions, noting that the front end of each runner stops 15mm (19/32in) short of the front edge of the two side panels, leaving room for the rails, and lies flush with the groove for the back panel.

Mix some wood glue and apply it to the four runners, butt-jointing them to the inside face of each side panel. Make certain that they are accurately located and allow plenty of time for the glue to harden fully.

The drawer rails are dowel-jointed to the side panels, using one 4mm (3/16in)-diameter dowel per joint, and the two side panels and back panel similarly joined to the base, using two 4mm (3/16in)-diameter dowels per panel. Mark in the positions of all the dowel holes with great accuracy and drill them out with a 4mm (3/16in)-diameter twist drill. The holes do not need to be drilled very deep, 6mm (1/4in) being quite sufficient.

Cut ten pieces of 4mm (3/16in)-diameter

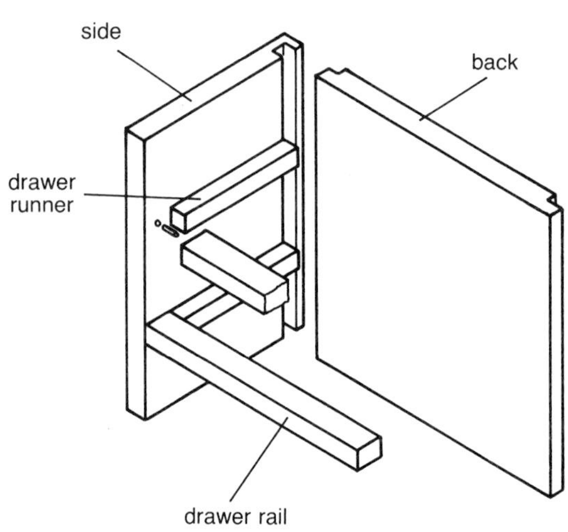

Exploded view of box components and joints.

The dowel joints are ready for assembly between the base and the two sides and back panel, with the drawer rails and runners already assembled in position.

The assembled sides and back are fitted to the base.

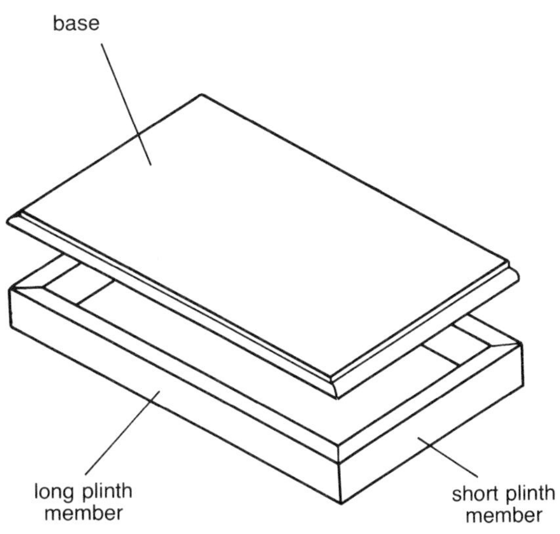

The plinth is made by mitre-jointing the long and short members together, and then glueing to the underside of the base.

dowelling to a length of 10mm (13/32in) each, mix more glue and apply it to the tongue and groove of the two lapped joints, the dowel joints and all three surfaces that butt up against one another between the three box panels and the base. Tap all the joints fully home with a small wooden mallet and place the assembly to one side for a day to dry completely.

Cut out the four lengths of 15×9mm (19/32×3/8in) material to form the plinth beneath the base panel, preparing mitre joints for each corner. Glue the four lengths to the underside of the base.

The lid is fastened to the back panel with two 25mm (1in) brass hinges, which are each set in and recessed 25mm (1in) from the sides of the box. It is usually best to fit the hinges in place with brass screws, but a word of caution here – tiny brass screws can easily shear as they are driven into their holes, so mark in the required positions of the holes with a panel pin, tapping it 2–3mm (3/32–1/8in) into the wood with a small hammer, and then drive in a small steel screw identical in size to the brass screws, to cut the thread. Now remove the steel screw and you will discover that each brass screw fits easily into its hole, avoiding the strain that could have broken it.

In the event that this technique should have the effect of cutting screw-holes that turn out to be too large, in which the brass screws fail to take a proper hold, simply apply a little adhesive to each screw as it is fitted.

The three identical drawers each consist of a drawer front cut from 9mm (3/8in)-thick material, and the two drawer sides and drawer back all cut from 6mm (1/4in)-thick wood. The drawer fronts

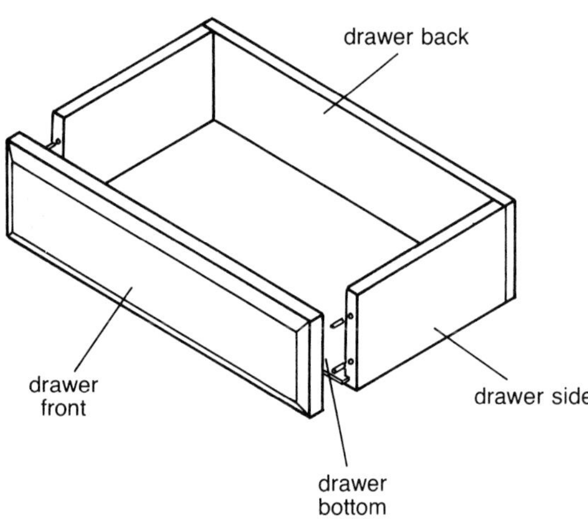

Drawer construction.

are given a decorative chamfered effect that is deliberately arranged to stand proud of the front surface of the box when the drawers are fitted in place.

Start by measuring and marking the drawer front to a length of 163mm (6⅜in) on a piece of 43×9mm (1¹⁹⁄₃₂×⅜in) material. Cut it to size with the jig-saw or tenon saw, taking care to ensure that the two ends are perfectly square. Next, mark in the areas to be chamfered. Bearing in mind that the thickness of the material is 9mm (⅜in), set the gap between the spur and the fence of the marking gauge to 7mm (⁹⁄₃₂in), hold the gauge so that the fence bears against the rear face of the drawer front, and scribe a line along the two edges and the two ends. Repeat the same marking for the other two drawer fronts. Take care to avoid putting too much pressure on the marking gauge, so that only a faint line is inscribed.

Re-set the gap between the spur and the fence to 5mm (⁷⁄₃₂in) and, holding the gauge this time with the fence bearing against the two edges and two ends, mark the faintest of lines in a rectangle on the front face of the drawer front. Clamp the material to the end of the workbench and remove the waste from the ends with a chisel, working it at a shallow angle to create the chamfer; and plane the slopes from the edges with the smoothing plane or spokeshave. Finish off with sandpaper.

Mark the two side panels and back panel for the drawer to the specified lengths. All four components for each drawer are now given a 2mm (³⁄₃₂in)-thick groove, set at 3mm (⅛in) from the bottom edge, to receive the thin plywood drawer bottom.

The groove is cut with a 2mm (³⁄₃₂in) veining cutter fitted to the router. It is cut continuously along the entire length of the side and back panels, but stopped 3mm (⅛in) short of the ends of the drawer front, so it is not visible when the drawer is finally assembled.

The cutting of the groove in the side and back panels will be greatly simplified if the router is worked along the strip of wood that measures 43×6mm (1¹¹⁄₁₆×¼in) before it is divided up into its marked lengths, so that you have sufficient material to clamp it to the workbench and can make a long run with the router, thus ensuring a more accurate groove.

Cut the side and back panels to length with the jig-saw, checking that the ends are absolutely square. The front and back panels are assembled to the drawer sides with dowel joints, using two 3mm (⅛in)-diameter dowels per joint. Prepare the drawer bottom from plywood measuring 152×93×2mm (6×3⅝×³⁄₃₂in), then mix some glue and assemble all three drawers.

A card template carries the pattern of hole markings for the dowel joints used in the drawer assembly, giving very accurate alignment of the component parts.

The drawer assembly is completed with the fitting of the drawer front.

Once the glue has dried, check that the drawers fit into their openings. The top drawer is fixed rigidly in place, but the other two should open and close easily. If you have measured accurately, the drawers should slide straight in – but it is always better for them to be slightly too large than too small, because they can be planed down until the fit is perfect.

Rub down the entire assembly with fine sandpaper and apply mahogany wood dye. When dry, give several applications of French polish until all the surfaces take on a rich glowing shine. Fit miniature brass drawer handles. These, like the small-diameter dowelling and very thin plywood, can be purchased from a modeller's shop. A range of handles and fittings can be obtained in 1/12th scale.

All three drawers are lined with velvet. The velvet is attached to a cardboard base that acts as an insert to the drawer and ensures that the fabric does not crease or wrinkle.

Measure the dimensions of the drawer interior and the distance between the plywood bottom and the top edge of the drawer. Transfer these measurements on to a piece of thick white card in such a way that by cutting a square from each corner and scoring four lines with a sharp knife, you can fold the sides up to form a rectangular box shape. If you have measured correctly and allowed for the thickness of the card, the box should just slide into the drawer. Trim the top edges of the card box so that they lie 2mm (3⁄32in) within the drawer.

Purchase some dress-making velvet and cut it slightly larger than the card. Then, with the card pressed out flat once again, stick it to the velvet with contact adhesive. Apply adhesive to the inside edges of the velvet and fold them over the edges of the card. Once dry, fold the card back into the shape of a box again and gently ease it down into the drawer until it is fully in place with only the velvet visible and nothing else.

Apply some wood glue to the runners of the top drawer to fix it permanently in position. Should you find either of the two opening drawers difficult to move in or out, rub a little candle wax on the top and bottom edges of the drawer sides to make the drawer run freely.

The card drawer insert is measured and cut to size, and a square of velvet prepared and stuck to it with contact adhesive.

Cutting List

Lid: one of 204×128×9mm (8×5×3⁄8in)
Base: one of 204×128×9mm (8×5×3⁄8in)
Side: two of 150×115×9mm (5 7⁄8×4 1⁄2×3⁄8in)
Back: one of 174×150×9mm (6 7⁄8×5 7⁄8×3⁄8in)
Drawer rail: two of 164×15×10mm (6 3⁄8×19⁄32×13⁄32in)
Drawer runner: four of 90×6×10mm (3 1⁄2×1⁄4×13⁄32in)
Drawer front: three of 163×43×9mm (6 3⁄8×1 19⁄32×3⁄8in)
Drawer side: six of 90×43×6mm (3 1⁄2×1 19⁄32×1⁄4in)
Drawer back: three of 163×43×6mm (6 3⁄8×1 19⁄32×1⁄4in)
Drawer bottom: three of 152×93×2mm (6×3 5⁄8×3⁄32in)
Long plinth member: two of 204×15×9mm (8×19⁄32×3⁄8in)
Short plinth member: two of 128×15×9mm (5×19⁄32×3⁄8in)

CHAPTER TEN

THE OVAL ROCKER

The oval rocker combines the features of the rocking horse and the see-saw, so that it can be used either by one child sitting in the middle facing either way, or by two children sitting at the ends and facing each other. Sturdy handgrips are provided, and the base of the rocker has a number of crosspieces, which not only give strength to the structure but also act as footrests to prevent the children's feet from slipping.

The design of the rocker is based on a geometrical pattern known as the ellipse, and it should be noted that both the sides and the seating panel are elliptical. The two sides are created from the smaller ellipse, which is then cut into two symmetrical halves along its major axis, whereas the seating panel is made from the larger ellipse, which is set in on both sides to provide adequate knee-room. The base panel is then cut and trimmed in such a way that it follows the same curved lines as those removed from the seating panel.

Although the rocker is quite straightforward in design and construction, the elliptical configuration does require spe-

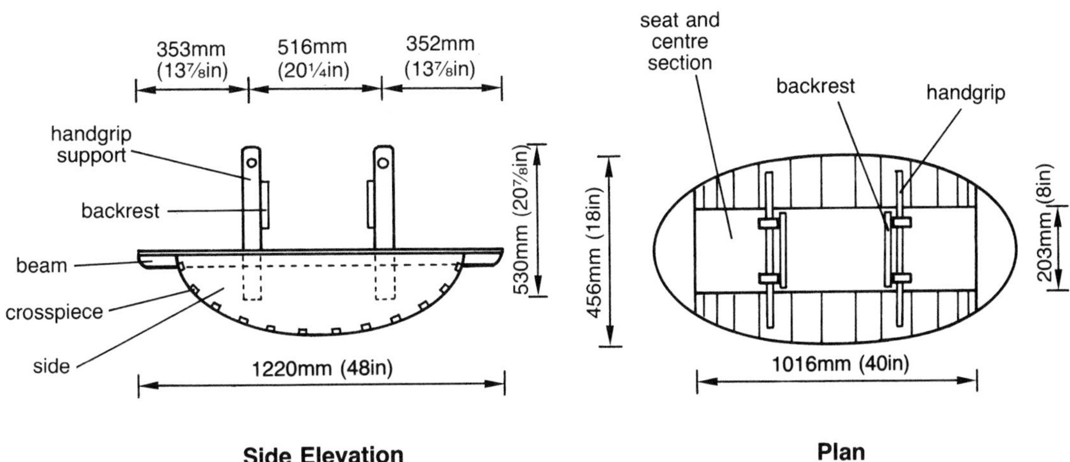

Main dimensions of the rocker.

cial attention, and even if a knowledge of geometry is not essential, it is important that you should know how to draw the ellipse with accuracy. There is no need to complicate the matter by using cardboard templates – the patterns may be drawn directly on to the plywood material.

Using birch-faced plywood of 13mm (½in) thickness, cut two rectangles, the first should exceed 1,220×456mm (48×18in) for the seating panel, and the second should exceed 1,016×760mm (40×30in) for the two side panels. Mark a cross on both pieces of plywood so that the two lines meet at right angles and intersect at the centre of each rectangle. These effectively form x and y coordinates, in which the x line is the shorter of the two lines, known as the minor axis, and the y line is the longer, or major axis.

Both ellipses may now be drawn on to the plywood using what is known as the trammel method. The trammel is simply a long strip of thin card with a perfectly straight edge, on to which three points are marked, these being referred to as P, x and y. Py is equal to half of the major axis and Px is equal to half of the minor axis. For marking out the seating panel, Py should be 610mm (24in) and Px 228mm (9in), and for the side panels, Py is 508mm (20in) and Px 380mm (15in).

To obtain the desired elliptical curve, lay the card trammel on the plywood so that x always touches the major axis and y always touches the minor axis. Make a small mark on the surface of the plywood in the P position, and work the trammel progressively around the four segments of the crossed lines until a complete ellipse is drawn. Sketch a pencil line between all the dots.

Cut round the curved lines with the jig-saw to remove the waste. In the case

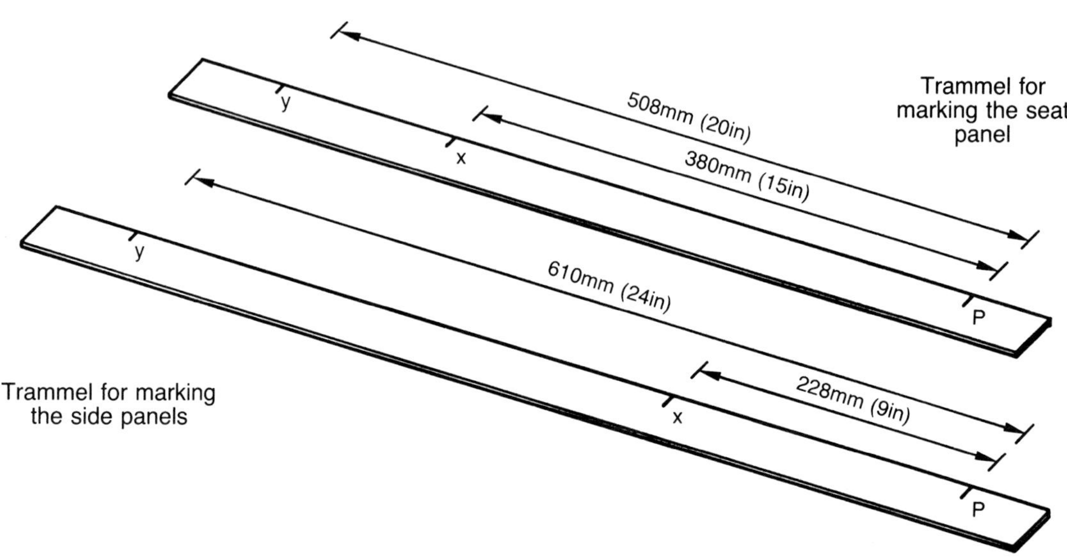

Marking out the P, x and y positions on the two cardboard trammels.

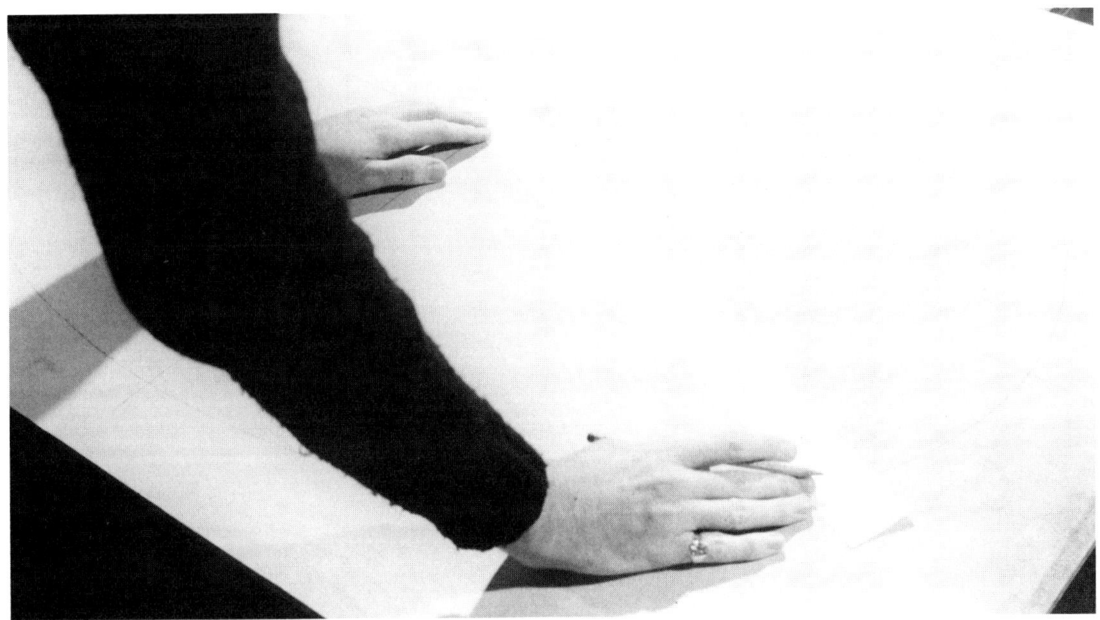

Mark the x and y axes on the panel and then work the trammel continuously between them, pencilling a series of dots in the P position to form an ellipse.

The two side panels are separated by cutting the plywood in half, and then cutting out the elliptical curves with the jig-saw.

The two side panels will not be perfectly identical when they are cut, so they should be placed against each other, clamped in the vice and their curved edges trimmed with the spokeshave until they are exactly the same shape.

of the smaller of the two ellipses, from which the side panels are derived, cut also along the major axis to split the ellipse into two equal halves. If necessary, clean up the straight edges with the smoothing plane and the curved edges with the spokeshave.

The next step is to measure and mark the setting in on both sides of the seating panel. The long rectangular centre section that runs between the two seats is 200mm (7⅞in) wide, and therefore the best way of marking this is by drawing two parallel lines in pencil, each of which is 100mm (4in) from the major axis. The rectangle is 1,016mm (40in) long, and this is established by similarly drawing two more lines, each being 508mm (20in) from the minor axis. Carefully remove the waste from the two sides with the jig-saw.

A series of notches must now be measured and marked along the curved edges of the two side panels, in precisely corresponding positions, to receive the twelve crosspieces. These should be arranged at regular intervals along both the curves. To find their exact location on the elliptical contour first cut a long strip of paper that is identical in length to the curved edge, and measure and mark in the crosspiece positions. As the crosspieces are cut from material measuring 25×13mm (1×½in), each notch must be 25mm (1in) wide and 13mm (½in) deep.

Transfer the twelve notch positions from the paper on to the sides, and mark in the rectangular waste areas. Prepare the notches by cutting away the waste with either the jig-saw or the coping saw, taking care to work the blade of the saw just to the waste side of the marked lines. Check the size of each notch by trying to fit a piece of 25×13mm (1×½in) material into it. If the notch is not quite large enough, trim the edges with a chisel until the wood just fits snugly inside.

Measure and mark the two long beams to a length of 1,220mm (48in) from 38×19mm (1½×¾in) beech. Because the seats are actually curved, the beams will be slightly too long, but for the time being they should be left as they are, and trimmed to their correct length after assembly has taken place.

Mix a fairly large quantity of wood glue and apply it by brush to the abutting surfaces between one side of the beam, and the inside upper surface of the side panel, in such a way that when the two parts are brought together, their upper edges lie flush with one another, and the beam projects by 100mm (4in) at each

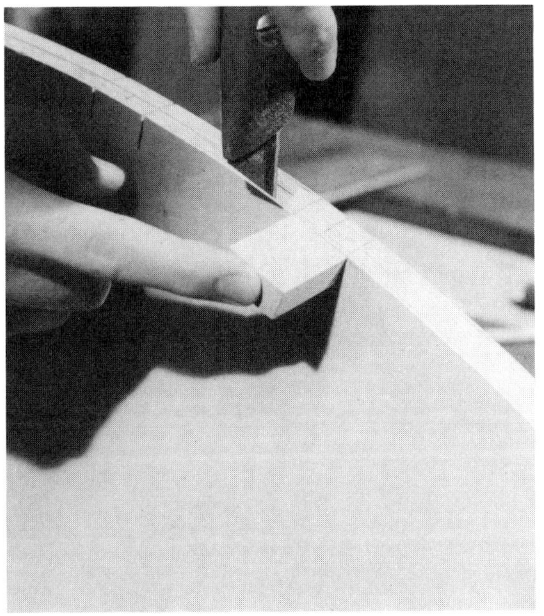

The two side panels are kept in exact alignment and the notch positions measured and marked. A small piece of scrap wood of the same cross-sectional dimensions as the crosspieces serves as a precise guide for the marking knife.

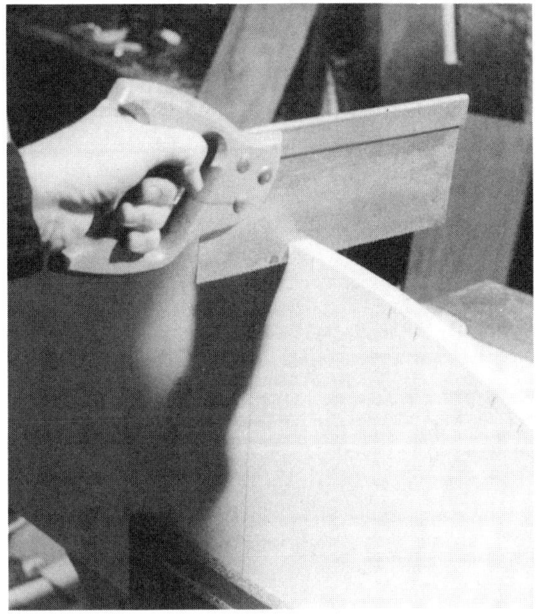

The notches are cut in both side panels simultaneously with the tenon saw.

end. Clamp the assembly together in several places, and wipe away any surplus glue with a damp cloth.

When the glue has dried completely, remove the clamps and strengthen the joint with six screws. Use 25mm (1in) number 8 countersunk woodscrews, arranging for the holes to be set at more or less regular intervals and drilled from the direction of the plywood into the beam. Note for later convenience, when assembling the hardgrip supports to the side panels, that the second and the fifth screw-holes should be set at a distance of 250mm (9⅞in) from either end. Fit a 25mm (1in) woodscrew in these holes for the moment. Later, when the handgrip supports are fitted, the holes will be enlarged for bigger screws.

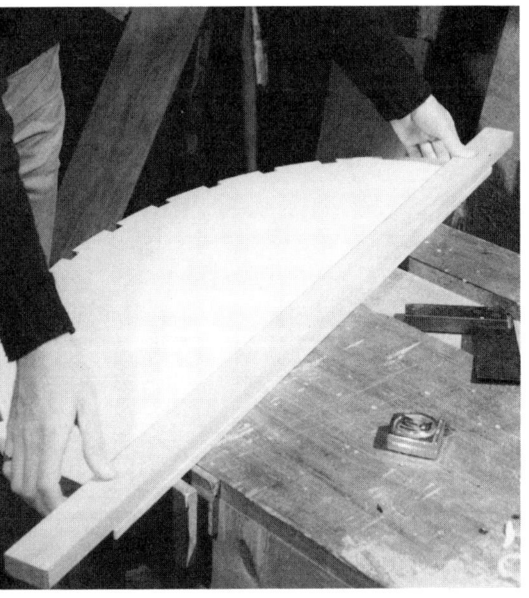

Mount the beam along the top edge of the side panel and mark their respective positions before assembling with wood glue and clamping the two parts firmly together.

The next stage is to proceed with the making of the four upright handgrip supports, each of which has a 19mm (¾in)-diameter hole drilled right through it to receive the dowelling that forms the handgrip. The supports must be fixed very securely to the rocker to ensure complete safety even when it is subjected to rough treatment, as a toy of this sort inevitably will be. Each of the four supports consists of a 530mm (20⅞in)-long piece of beech, measuring 45x19mm (1¾×¾in) in cross-sections of which 380mm (15in) of its length projects above the top edge of the sides.

Measure the four supports to length, rounding off the top end with pair of geometrical compasses set to a radius of 22mm (⅞in), and marking in the position of the 19mm (¾in)-diameter hole through which the handgrip will pass, setting this 32mm (1¼in) down from the top. Square off the bottom end. Then, before cutting the supports to size, drill out each handgrip hole using a 19mm (¾in)-diameter centre bit, stopping when the point of the bit just breaks through on the opposite side, and turning the wood over to complete the drilling.

Mark in the curved upper end of the handgrip supports with a pair of compasses.

Clamp the wood firmly at the side of the workbench and cut the rounded end with the jig-saw or the coping saw, and the squared end with the tenon saw. Finally, place all four supports together to check that they are of equal length and that their handgrip holes coincide exactly. If not, adjust them slightly so that the holes are level, and then, after passing a length of 19mm-diameter dowelling through the four holes to keep them in alignment, trim the ends at the bottom.

The handgrip supports are mounted to the inside surface of the two side panels, but as these already each have a beam fitted in place measuring 19mm (¾in) in thickness, a spacer block of the same thickness must be attached to the lower portion of the four supports. Since the supports are required to project by 380mm (15in) above the sides, and the beams are each 38mm (1½in) wide, it follows that each of the spacers must be 112mm (4⅜in) long, 45mm (1¾in) wide and 19mm (¾in) thick.

The spacer is butt-jointed to the side of the handgrip support in such a way that their bottom ends are perfectly flush with one another. Mix some wood glue, apply it to the joining surfaces, and clamp the two parts firmly together until the glue has dried thoroughly.

The four combined handgrip supports and spacers must now be affixed to the

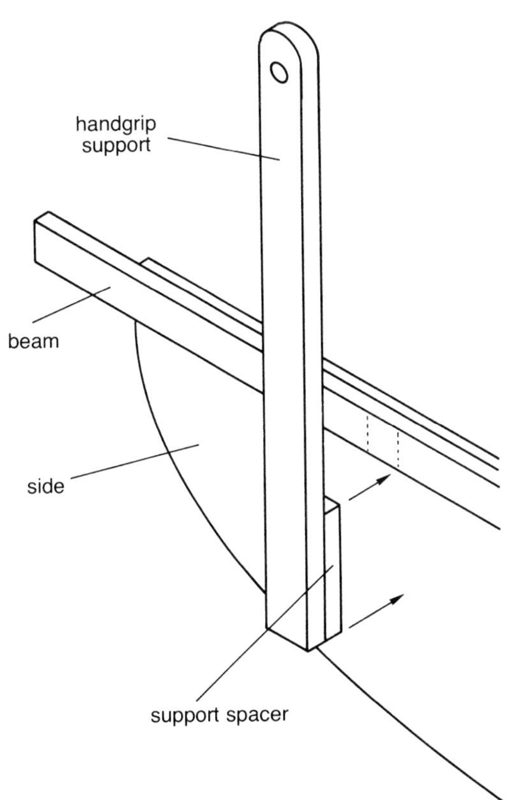

Assembling the handgrip support and spacer to inside surface of the side panel.

The four rectangular holes for the handgrip supports must be measured and marked accurately in the seat panel and then cut out with the jig-saw.

inside surface of the two side panels, each support being mounted in a vertical position 250mm (9⅞in) from the end. Once again, the joint should initially be assembled with wood glue, the glue being applied to the outer face of the spacer block and to a correspondingly marked line on the inside of the plywood, and the glue joint reinforced with two 50mm (2in) number 8 countersunk woodscrews. As an additional means of securing the handgrip support, a further 50mm (2in) screw should be driven through the hole already made in the plywood and the beam, and presently occupied by a 25mm (1in) woodscrew. Remove this screw, drill the hole a little deeper, so that the bit bores into the support, and fit the 50mm (2in) screw instead.

At the four positions where the handgrip supports project above the top edge of the two side panels, four rectangular holes must be cut into the long centre section between the seats, to coincide exactly. So each hole should measure 46×20mm (1 13/16×13/16in), this being fractionally greater than the cross-section of the supports. Measure the four positions for the holes on the plywood with accuracy, and remove the waste from each one by firstly drilling through the middle of the marked-out area with a 16mm (⅝in)-diameter centre bit, and then introducing

Check that the crosspieces fit into their receiver holes in the side panels before commencing assembly.

the blade of the jig-saw or coping saw and working it towards all four corners before taking out successively larger pieces of waste until the blade can be worked along each of the marked lines.

Check that the hole is sufficiently big to admit the handgrip support, and if not, file down the sides of the hole until the wood slips through.

Cut the twelve crosspieces from 25×13mm (1×½in) beech, each measuring 456mm (18in) long. Although the crosspieces and the attached base panel will eventually assume a curved shape that follows the original elliptical pattern of the seats, it is much easier to start by cutting and fitting them when they are all of an equal length, and trimming them to their correct size later.

Once these have been prepared, twenty-four triangular joining blocks must be made from any left-over hardwood. First, cut twelve cubes, each measuring 25×25×25mm (1×1×1in), then saw these diagonally to produce the required number of triangles. During the assembling of the rocker, the blocks are used to strengthen the joints between the side panels and the crosspieces, and are mounted on the inside where they are concealed from view. The plywood, of course, is not of sufficient thickness to make a good joint on its own.

Prepare for the assembly of the rocker in the following way. Start by checking the width of the centre section between the seats, which sould be 200mm (7⅞in). Taking each of the twelve crosspieces, mark a point at the centre of each one, and then measure a line 100mm (4in) to one side and a line 100mm (4in) to the other side, so that the two lines are set 200mm (7⅞in) apart. Mark in the two lines with the try-square.

Now mix a large amount of wood glue, and apply it by brush to the inside edges of all the notches, fitting the crosspieces in place so that the squared lines are just

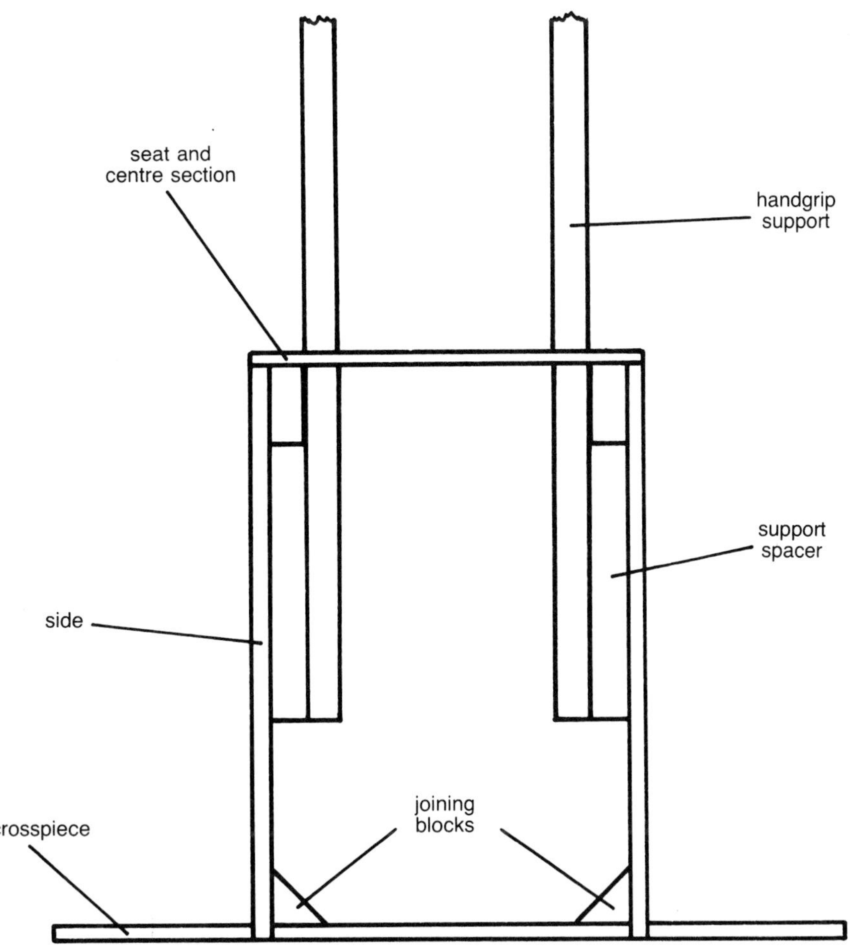

Cross-sectional view showing the positions of the reinforcing triangular joining blocks.

visible on the outside surfaces of the two side panels. When all of the crosspieces are in position, assemble the joining blocks to the sides and the crosspieces with glue.

Next, apply glue along the upper edge of the two long beams, and lay the seat panel in place, pinning it down with very thin panel pins.

When the glue has set, strengthen the joint between the seat panel and the two beams by driving twelve 25mm (1in) number 8 woodscrews through the plywood into each beam, arranging the screws at regular intervals.

When the main assembly is complete, the next stage is to cut and fit the base panel. This will need to be very flexible, in order to follow the rather tight curves at each end of the sides, adjoining the seats. Plywood of 4mm (3⁄16in) thickness should be used, the width being not

Glue the twelve crosspieces into their receiver notches.

greater than 456mm (18in). The overall length of the panel may be determined by using the long strip of paper that was used to mark out the notches as a convenient guide, or by running a piece of string around the curved edge of one side panel, and allowing a little extra at each end for a slight overlap with the seats.

Mark the strip of paper, or the piece of string, and set it against a tape measure to give the required length of the base panel. Before it can be fitted, two notches will have to be cut at either end to fit around the beams, and a shallow recess cut to a width of 456mm (18in) for the ends of the base to fit around the centre section.

Soak the plywood thoroughly with water to make it pliable, and then, with the assistance of one or two people, bend it into position. If the two ends of the base panel can be made to butt loosely up against the seats, this should help to hold it roughly in place as the plywood gradually dries out. When all the moisture has gone, the panel should retain some of its newly-acquired curvature, making the next step much easier.

Temporarily detach the base from the rocker assembly, mix a large guantity of wood glue, and apply it to all the joining surfaces between the undersides of the crosspieces, the curved edges of the side panels and the straight edges of the two seats. Fit the base back into position and tack it down with panel pins. When the glue has dried, reinforce the assembly with woodscrews, driving in at least four 19mm (¾in) number 8 countersunk woodscrews through the plywood of the base panel into the crosspieces.

Where the ends of the base reach beyond the seats, trim back with the plane until they are neatly flush.

Finally, mark the curvature on both sides of the base to make it conform to the original elliptical pattern marked on the seating panel. This is rather a difficult task because the base is steeply curved at each end, and the elliptical pattern can only really be marked by eye, using something flexible like a piece of string, which is laid on the base in an appropriate manner and then pencilled in. Remove the waste from the base and the crosspieces with the coping saw and the spokeshave. The spokeshave will be responsible for refining the curves on both sides, and you must judge with your own eye when they match up with each other.

Trim both ends of the two beams to match them to the contour of the seats, and round off the bottom corners with the spokeshave to give a better contact with the ground when the rocker is in use.

Cut two pieces of 19mm (¾in)-diameter dowelling to a length of 380mm (15in), and assemble these through the holes in the handgrip supports with wood glue, adjusting their positions so that approximately 110mm (4⁵⁄₁₆in) projects on either side.

Simple backrests may be made from 13mm (½in)-thick plywood, measuring 162x100mm (6⅜x4in), and mounted on the inside edges of the handgrip supports, so that a child can sit on the inside of the rocker, facing either direction, and have something to lean back against. Indeed, if you wish, these backrests could be padded with small cushions made from pieces of foam covered in plastic, and attached to the backrests with ties or pop-fasteners.

The rocker can either be painted, varnished or treated with a water-resistant outdoor finish, depending on whether it is to be played with inside the house or out in the garden. A colourful paint scheme would certainly be the brightest and most attractive idea, but not necessarily the most practical!

Cutting List

Side: two of 1016×380×13mm (40×15×½in)
Seat and centre section: one of 1220×456×13mm (48×18×½in)
Beam: two of 1220×38×19mm (48×1½×¾in)
Handgrip support: four of 530×45×19mm (20⅞×1¾×¾in)
Support spacer: four of 112×45×19mm (4⅜×1¾×¾in)
Crosspiece: twelve of 456×25×13mm (18×1×½in)
Base: one of 1430×456×4mm (56¼×18×³⁄₁₆in)
Backrest: two of 162×100×13mm (6⅜×4×½in)
Handgrip: two of 380×19mm (15×¾in) diameter

Chapter Eleven

The Castle Toy Box

This is a castle with a practical purpose, for when it is not playing the role of a medieval fortress, it can be used to store lots of toys. At first, it may appear to be no more than a simple box suitably decorated with castellated towers and parapets, with a recessed lid allowing access to the interior; but, in addition, there are slitted windows in the towers, each with a small ledge to support defending soldiers, and the main entrance has a drawbridge connected to a portcullis by two chains, so that when the drawbridge is lowered the portcullis goes up and when the drawbridge is raised, the portcullis comes down. A thin shutter slides into a slot behind the portcullis to enclose the box when it is being used for storing other toys.

CONSTRUCTING THE BOX

The first stage is to construct the box.

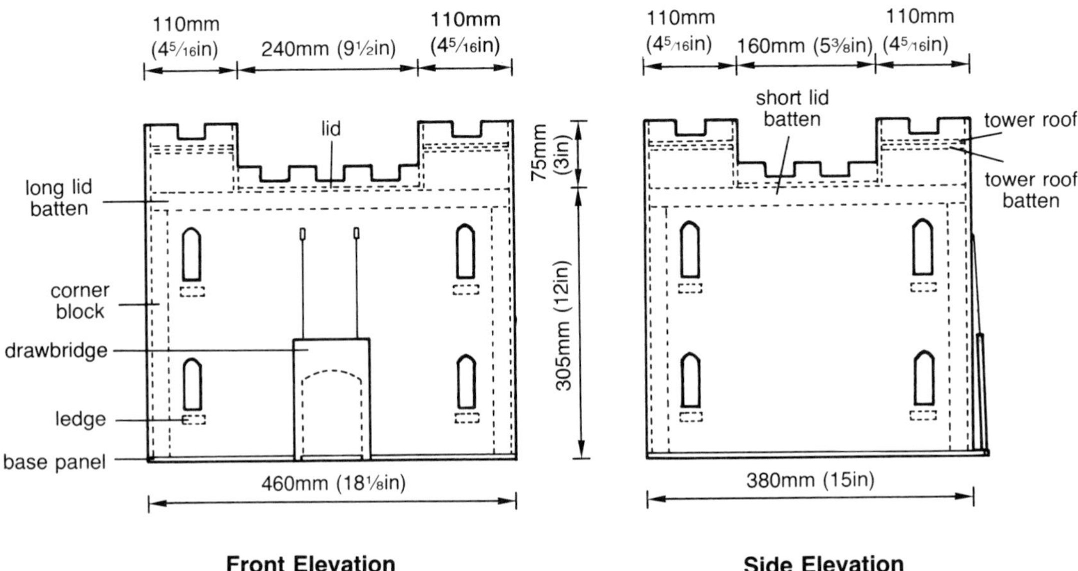

Main dimensions of castle toy box.

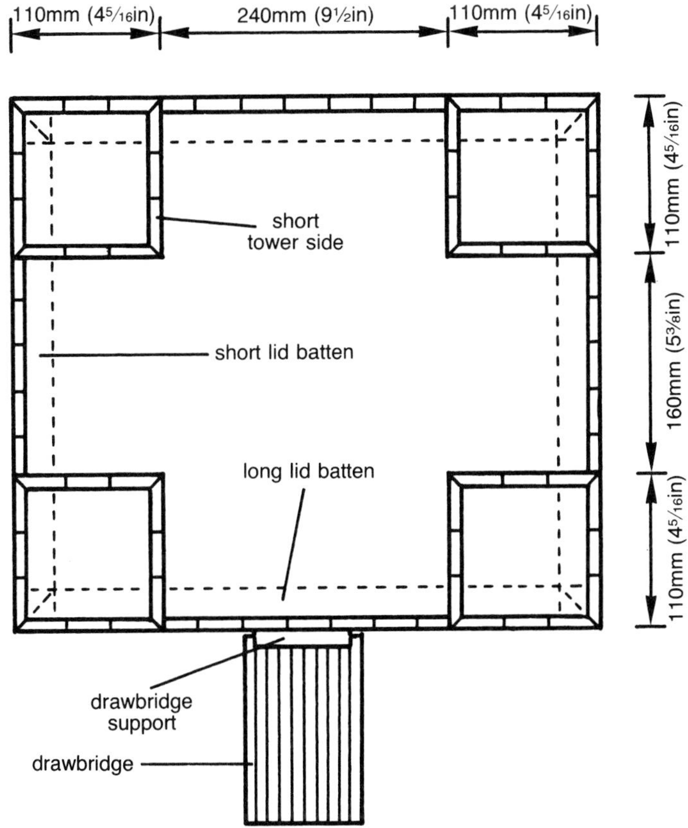

Plan of castle toy box.

This consists of a base with four walls. At each corner of the box, at the top, a square tower is built, and in between these four towers, in the shape of a large cross, is the lid of the box. Each of these components is cut from 9mm (⅜in)-thick birch-faced plywood.

Start by preparing the base. Measure and mark a rectangle on the 9mm (⅜in) plywood whose length is 460mm (18⅛in) and width is 380mm (15in). Use set-squares to make sure that each corner forms a perfect right angle. Cut the board to size with the jig-saw, taking great care to keep the blade working in an absolutely straight line, cutting on the waste side of the four pencil lines.

It is, of course, almost impossible to guarantee that a hand-held saw will remain accurately aligned throughout the entire cut, so each edge should be lightly planed afterwards to smooth out any small irregularities.

Measure and mark the front, back and two side panels to size from 9mm (⅜in)-thick plywood, initially marking out rectangles of 460×380mm (18⅛×15in) for the front and the back, and rectangles

Clamp the front panel securely to the workbench and cut out the recessed parapet and crenellations with the jig-saw.

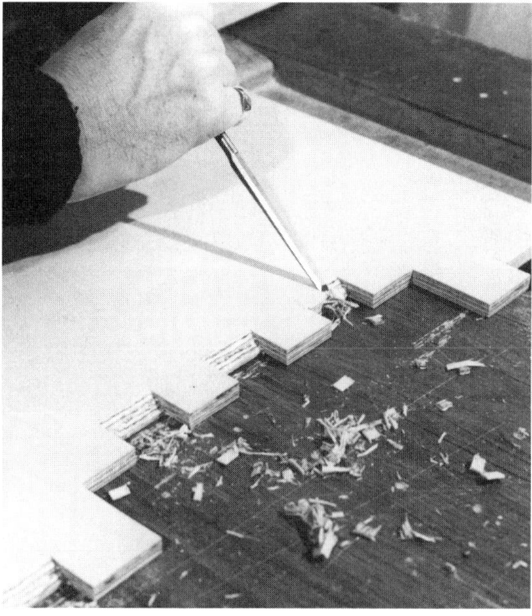

The inside edges of the embrasures are bevelled by firstly sawing angled cuts with the hacksaw and paring away the waste with the chisel.

measuring 380×380mm (15×15in) for the sides. Now measure and mark in the castellated towers and the crenellated parapets, following the general dimensions that allow for the towers being 110mm (4 5/16in) wide, so that the gap between them will be 240mm (9 7/16in) for the front and back panels and 160mm (6 9/32in) for the two side panels. The parapet is recessed by 50mm (2in) below the tops of the towers for all four panels.

Mark in the crenellations at the tops of the towers and along the parapets. These should be approximately 32mm (1¼in) wide and 16mm (⅝in) deep, arranged centrally across the width of each tower, and at regular intervals along the parapets.

Cut out each panel with the jig-saw, concentrating firstly on the main dimensions, then cutting out the recess for the parapet, and, finally, each of the crenellations. Strictly speaking, these should each have bevelled embrasures, meaning that in each case all three edges are sloped so that the openings are wider on the inside surfaces of the tower and the parapet, so that the defenders behind the walls could gain a better view without exposing themselves to attack. The degree of bevelling need only be slight, and may be cut by sawing with the hacksaw and paring away the waste with the chisel.

Mark in the doorway and window openings on the front panel, and window openings only on the two side panels and back panel noting that these are arranged to coincide with the towers. All the windows are long and narrow,

Cut out the arched entrance and window openings with the jig-saw.

with Gothic arches at the top; the door opening is similarly arched. The exact size and position of the windows is not so important, but the door opening should measure 100mm (4in) high by 70mm (2¾in) wide, and be located centrally with respect to the front panel. Cut out all of the openings with the jig-saw or coping saw; in the case of the windows, a hole will firstly have to be drilled through the marked area with an auger bit to give access for the saw blade.

Mark out and cut the two openings for the drawbridge chains. These are set 70mm (2¾in) apart, so that they line up with the sides of the door frame and are located 260mm (10¼in) up from the bottom edge of the panel. Each opening should measure 13mm (½in) high by 7mm (9/32in) wide, and is cut by boring through the plywood with a 6mm (¼in)-diameter auger bit in two positions, one above the other, both within the marked rectangle, and then chopping out the remaining waste with a 6mm chisel and mallet. These openings will accommodate a small roller over which the chain for the drawbridge and portcullis passes.

The method of joining the four wall panels to the base is by the lapped joint, in which a rebate measuring 9mm (⅜in) wide and 4mm (3/16in) deep is cut on the upper surface of the base against each of the four edges. There are various ways in which the rebate can be prepared: the quickest way is to employ an electric router fitted with a rebating cutter, and the tool suitably adjusted to produce the required amount of cut; or the plough plane may be used, fitted with a 9mm (⅜in) cutter and a special adapter plate for the plough to cut across the grain; or you can simply saw carefully along each marked line with the tenon saw, cutting down to a depth of 4mm (3/16in), and chisel away the waste.

The four wall panels are mitre-jointed at each corner for neatness and the mitres reinforced with wooden joining blocks. Once again, there is more than one way of preparing a mitre joint: if you have an electric router available, fit it with a 45-degree grooving cutter and line it up carefully against the side where the bevel is to be cut – having clamped the panel securely to the surface of the workbench – and run the router against the edge of the piece. It may be necessary to take two or more runs before the desired mitre is achieved, but take great care not to over-cut, otherwise the panel will be fractionally shortened. An alternative method is to mark in the mitres with a 45-degree mitre square, and gradually chisel away all the waste. This will take time

Mitre-joint the four wall panels by working the router, fitted with a 45-degree grooving cutter, along the inner surface of each joining edge.

but the result should be equally effective.

When all the mitres have been cut, make a trial fitting of the four panels to the base to ensure that they come together neatly.

The Towers

The next step is to prepare the two short sides for each tower, which should measure 110×75mm (4⁵⁄₁₆×3in). Before cutting these to length, however, note that they also have mitres cut along both edges. If you are using the electric router to machine the 45-degree bevels, the preparation will be much simplified by cutting a single piece of plywood, measuring 110mm (4⁵⁄₁₆in) along the grain, and 600mm (23⅝in) wide – preferably more than this, to allow a margin for cutting the piece up into eight sections of 75mm (3in) width – and working the router along both the sides. Such a wide piece of plywood will be much easier to clamp to the end of the workbench than eight small pieces.

When each short side panel has been mitred and cut to size, mark the crenellations at the top and cut them out with the coping saw and the chisel.

Taking each tower in turn, select two short sides and mark on each one the 50mm (2in) length of mitre that matches that of the tower on the main panels before the level of the parapet is reached. Beneath the level of the parapet the mitred portion should be cut away leaving a squared edge that butts up against the inside surface of the main panel. At the same time, mark in the corresponding mitre that must be cut on the 50mm (2in) length of tower on the main panel, and trim off the waste with the tenon saw or chisel. The router would be unsuitable for such a short cut.

Each tower has a flat roof recessed 16mm (⅝in) below the top edge, consisting of a square piece of 9mm (⅜in)-thick plywood measuring 92×92mm (3⅝×3⅝in). Support battens, each measuring 92×9×9mm (3⅝×⅜×⅜in), are prepared from hardwood strip, with a mitre joint cut at each end, and these are glued to the inside surface of all four tower walls, with their upper edge located 25mm (1in) from the top edge. Measure and mark their positions with accuracy, so that they are all set at the same level.

At the same time, cut short ledges from 25×13mm hardwood strips each measuring 25mm (1in) in length, and glue these in position 6mm (¼in) below the windows on the inside surface of the front and two side panels, so that toy soldiers can be arranged to stand behind all the windows.

ASSEMBLY

The main components of the castle are now ready for assembly. Mix a large quantity of strong wood glue and apply it by brush to all four rebates cut in the base. Now take the front, back and two side panels and apply glue to all the mitre joints, and to the bottom edge of each panel. Place them one by one on to the base until all the joints are in close contact. So that the joints stay tightly together while the glue dries, cut four 300mm (11¹³⁄₁₆in) lengths of 19×19mm (¾×¾in) L-shaped corner square moulding, line the inside of each one with a thin strip of newspaper, and fit them over the corners of the castle so that two string tourniquets can be applied without the risk of the string cutting into the plywood. Inevitably, some of the glue will squeeze out of the joints but, after a day or so when the tourniquets are removed, only the newspaper will be stuck to the corners of the castle, and this can be removed by scraping off with a sharp chisel and rubbing down with sandpaper.

Begin assembling the box by applying glue to the rebated base, then fit the front panel in position, followed by one side, continuing until the box structure is complete.

Complete the four towers by applying more glue to the joints and fitting the short sides and the recessed flat roof. These should similarly be bound together with string tourniquets, and each 300mm (11¹³⁄₁₆in) piece of L-shaped corner square moulding can be cut up into four lengths of 75mm (3in), equal to the height of the towers.

Glue the four lid battens in position and hold them firmly with clamps while the glue dries and hardens.

To reinforce the corners of the castle, cut four pieces of 19×19mm (¾×¾in) ramin, each measuring 282mm (11⅛in) long, apply glue to two adjacent edges and press them firmly into the corners, holding them in place by wedging thin wooden struts diagonally across the inside of the box. It is important that you measure and cut each one accurately to length, because this will leave a gap of 19mm (¾in) between the top end of these corner blocks and the bottom edges of the short sides of the four towers. Into these gaps fit four lengths of 19×19mm (¾×¾in) ramin so that they lie horizontally, two measuring 442mm (17⅜in) long to reach across the inside width of the front and back panel, and two measuring 362mm (14¼in) long to reach across the inside width of the two side panels. Where the battens meet, their corners must be mitre-jointed before gluing them in position. Assuming that the upright corner blocks have been cut to the correct length, these four horizontal battens should just slide into place and rest on top of the blocks.

THE LID

The battens provide a support for the lid of the box and, although it is not intended for standing on, the structure should safely support a child's weight as the battens rest on the corner blocks

The lid of the box must be fitted with a handle or knob, to facilitate easy removal. Remember that the hand grip must be suitable for a young child to grasp safely.

that run down as far as the base. Note that the battens are recessed below the castellated parapets, leaving room for the lid to be placed in position.

Mark out the lid on a piece of 9mm ($\frac{3}{8}$in)-thick plywood. Start by measuring a rectangle of 442×362mm ($17\frac{3}{8}\times14\frac{1}{4}$in), using set-squares to ensure that each corner forms a perfect right angle, and mark a square at all four corners measuring 101×101mm (4×4in) equal to the space occupied by the towers. Cut out the rectangle with the jig-saw, planing the edges so that they are smooth and square, and, finally, cut away the waste portions from the corners. Before the lid can be fitted in place on top of the castle, a wooden handle or knob must be fixed at the centre on its upper surface, otherwise it will be difficult to remove.

The construction of the castle is now finished and it only remains to make the drawbridge and portcullis, although these could be omitted if you prefer the simplicity of the box by itself. However, they do add an authentic touch and make the castle much more exciting to play with.

THE DRAWBRIDGE

The drawbridge is made by gluing together ten strips of 9×9mm ($\frac{3}{8}\times\frac{3}{8}$in) ramin. The outer two strips measure 130mm ($5\frac{1}{8}$in) long and the remaining eight measure 115mm ($4\frac{1}{2}$in) in length. They are arranged in such a way that their ends are all flush at the outer extremity, so that at the opposite end the eight lengths are set in by 15mm ($\frac{15}{32}$in)

The ten components of the drawbridge are cut and butt-jointed together.

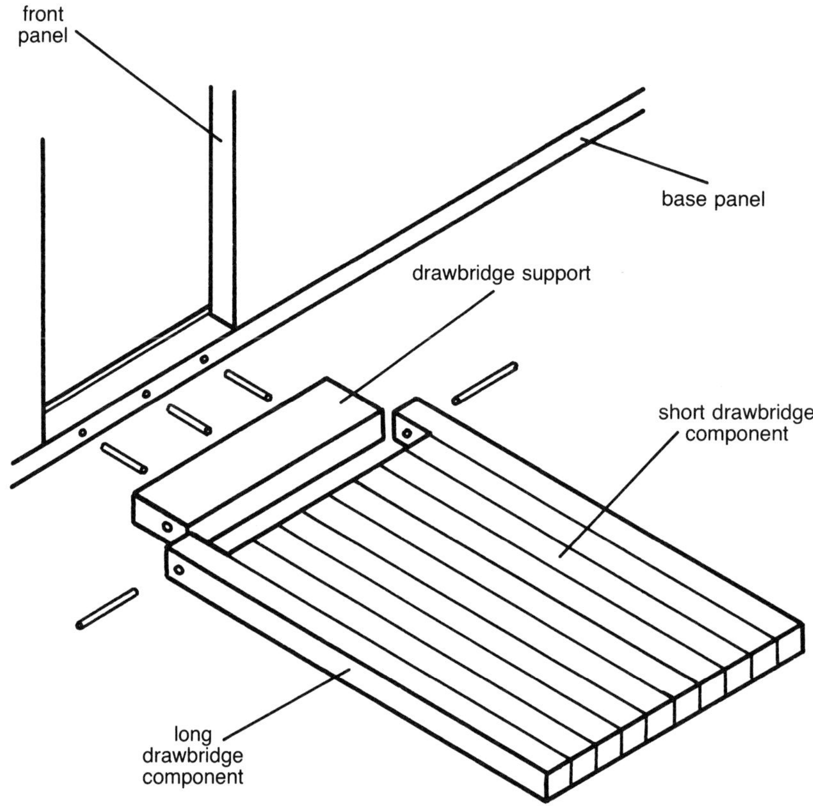

Exploded drawbridge and support assembly.

from the outside pieces. Before assembling the ten lengths edge to edge with glue, chamfer their corners slightly to provide a V-shaped groove between each strip, and drill a 2mm (3⁄32in)-diameter hole through the projecting outside pieces to receive the steel axle rod that will be used to hinge the drawbridge to its support.

This support is cut from a piece of ramin trimmed to 70×19×9mm (2¾×¾×⅜in), which has two 2mm (3⁄32in)-diameter holes drilled in corresponding positions in both the end-grains: these holes may either be drilled to meet halfway along the length of the support, and thus pass right through it, or they can both be bored to a depth of 19mm (¾in), the hinge pin being cut to an overall length of 90mm (3½in) in the former case, or into two lengths of 28mm (1⅛in) each in the latter.

The support is attached to the front edge of the base panel and occupies the position directly in front of the door opening, the length of the support being identical to the width of the doorway. It should be dowel-jointed in place, using three dowels of 4–5mm (3/16–7/32in) diameter, the receiver holes being drilled to a depth of 9mm (3/8in). Apply glue also to the two abutting surfaces to ensure a strong joint, because the drawbridge will be subjected to a great deal of wear.

THE PORTCULLIS

The portcullis is made from a piece of 110×88mm (4 5/16×3 7/16in) plywood of 6mm (1/4in)-thickness, a pattern of squares being drawn on one side and cut out with a drill-bit and jig-saw or coping saw. The portcullis is always pronged at the bottom. Mounted behind the portcullis is a protective shutter, also cut from 6mm (1/4in) plywood, measuring 260×88mm (10 1/4×3 7/16in), the purpose of which is to shield the portcullis and its lifting mechanism from damage caused by the storage of toys inside the box.

Both the portcullis and the shutter are housed in grooves cut in two upright columns attached to the inside surface of the front panel, on either side of the door opening. The columns are prepared from 25×25mm (1×1in) ramin, and each one has a rebate cut in the corner to a width of 9mm (3/8in) and a depth of 7mm (9/32in), to receive the portcullis, and a groove of similar dimensions set 6mm (1/4in) behind, to receive the shutter. The two columns are cut to a length of 230mm (9in) and butt-jointed to the inside of the front panel with wood glue. They must, of course, be parallel and vertical.

The drawbridge is connected to the portcullis by means of two thin chains that are attached to screw-eyes set in the top edge of the portcullis and to the upper

Mark the portcullis pattern on to a piece of plywood, and bore a 6mm (1/4in) diameter hole through each of the squared openings.

Cut the squared openings of the portcullis carefully to shape with the jig-saw or coping saw.

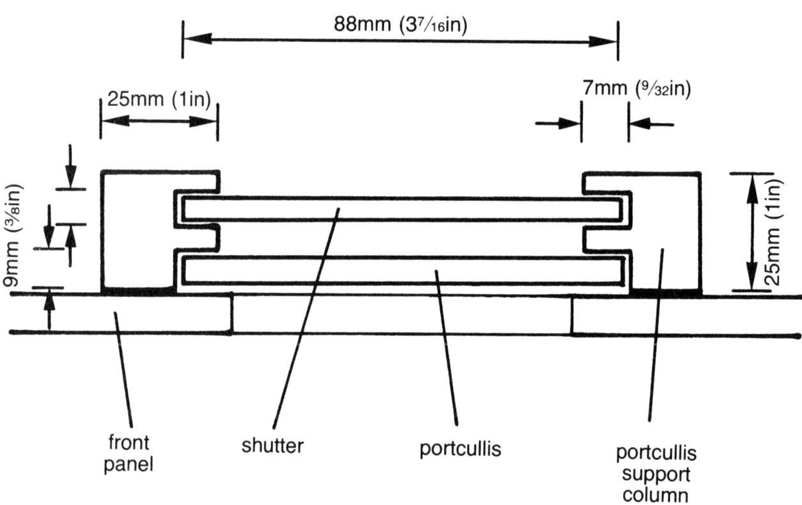

Method of mounting the portcullis and shutter to the front panel.

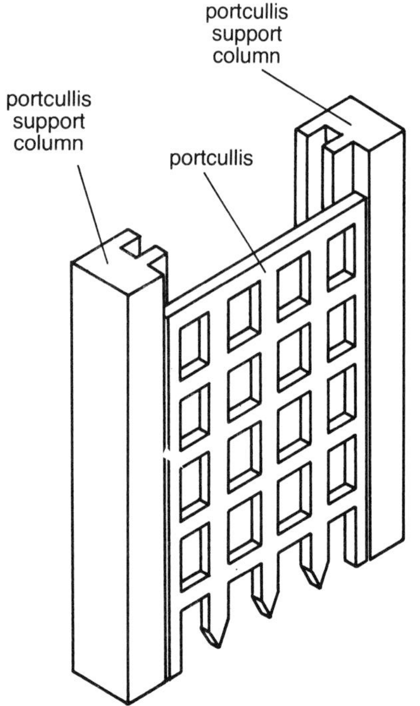

Portcullis set in grooves cut in two upright support columns.

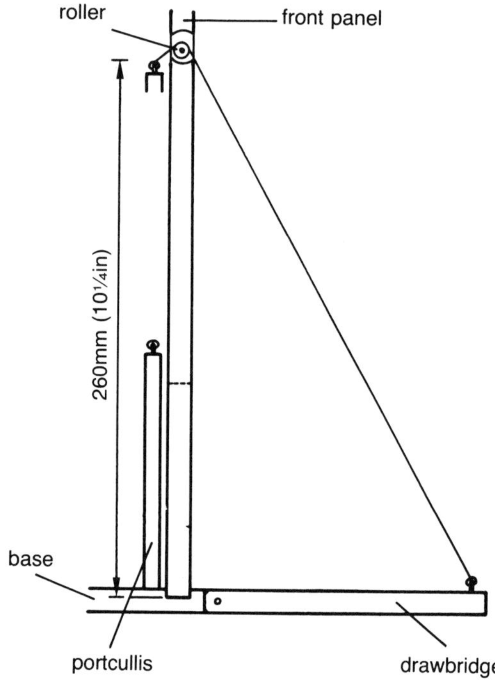

Drawbridge/portcullis mechanism.

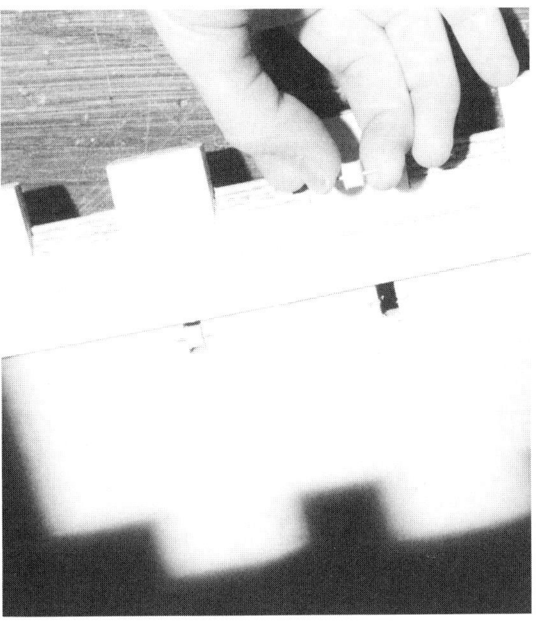

Mount the two rollers for the drawbridge chains into their openings.

surface of the drawbridge, 10mm (13/32in) from the far end. The chain material and the four screw-eyes can be obtained from a model shop. Where the chain passes through the two narrow holes above the door opening, its movement will be made much freer if it passes over rollers set inside the openings. If you break open an old audio cassette tape you will find that there are two small plastic rollers of just the right size, which can be mounted on veneer pins, cut to a length of 13mm (½in) with a pair of pliers and fitted into tiny slits cut with a sharp knife into the wood on either side of the two holes, and held in place with adhesive.

The length of chain can only be determined by dropping the portcullis and raising the drawbridge, attaching the chain to the screw-eyes on the portcullis, passing them over the rollers and finding the links that align with the level of the drawbridge screw-eyes.

FINISHING TOUCHES

It only remains to paint the castle in a light grey colour, with dark brown for the drawbridge and portcullis. A darker shade of grey could be used for the door and window openings and for the crenellations on the towers and the parapets.

Cutting List

Base: one of 460×380×9mm (18⅛×15×⅜in)
Front panel: one of 460×380×9mm (18⅛×15×⅜in)
Back panel: one of 460×380×9mm (18⅛×15×⅜in)
Side panel: two of 380×380×9mm (15×15×⅜in)
Lid: one of 442×362×9mm (17⅜×14¼×⅜in)
Short tower side: eight of 110×75×9mm (4 5/16×3×⅜in)
Tower flat roof: four of 92×92×9mm (3⅝×3⅝×⅜in)
Corner block: four of 282×19×19mm (11⅛×¾×¾in)
Lid batten, long: two of 442×19×19mm (17⅜×¾×¾in)
Lid batten, short: two of 362×19×19mm (14¼×¾×¾in)
Tower roof batten: sixteen of 92×9×9mm (3⅝×⅜×⅜in)
Drawbridge, long component: two of 130×9×9mm (5⅛×⅜×⅜in)
Drawbridge, short component: eight of 115×9×9mm (4½×⅜×⅜in)
Drawbridge support: one of 70×19×9mm (2¾×¾×⅜in)
Portcullis: one of 110×88×6mm (4 5/16×3 7/16×¼in)
Shutter: one of 260×88×6mm (10¼×3 7/16×¼in)
Portcullis support column: two of 230×25×25mm (9×1×1in)

CHAPTER TWELVE

THE FARM TRACTOR AND CART

Children are usually fascinated by the farmyard, and agricultural machinery seems to hold a special attraction. This farm tractor and cart set is easily constructed from small blocks of wood and pieces of thin plywood and, in common with many of the other toys described in this book, the material needed can be obtained from odds and ends left over from other work.

The choice of wood is not particularly important, except to say that it ought to be a hardwood; beyond that, the type of hardwood depends very much on what you can find lying around the workshop. This example is made from oak and birch-faced ply.

THE WHEELS

The first step is to cut the wheels to shape. Those attached to the tractor are in two different sizes: the large wheels at the back being 50mm (2in) in diameter, whereas the small wheels at the front are of 28mm (1⅛in) diameter. All four wheels on the cart are the same as the small front wheels of the tractor – 28mm (1⅛in) in diameter. Each wheel is of the same 19mm (¾in) thickness, except for the pair at the front of the tractor, which are 13mm (½in) thick.

There are several ways of cutting out circular discs of wood, but the method used here is to employ a saw specially designed for cutting round holes. The blade is cylindrical, and various diameters are available. They are mounted

Cut the wheels from a block of oak, using a cylindrical saw blade mounted, in this case, in an electric drill.

on to a circular plate that has a number of concentric grooves, with a long twist-drill type of bit at the centre to serve as a guide, positioning the saw correctly before the blade begins to cut.

Fit a cylindrical blade of 50mm (2in) diameter – or as near to this as possible – into the circular plate, mount the assembly into a handbrace or electric drill, and start drilling with the pilot bit through a piece of 19mm (¾in)-thick oak, which should be clamped firmly to the end of the workbench. As the cylindrical blade makes contact with the surface of the wood and begins to cut through it, keep applying firm effort to the drill, making sure that it remains perpendicular to the wood at all times, until you estimate that you have cut approximately halfway through. By this time, the pilot bit will have passed right through the thickness of the wood.

Turn the piece of oak over, once again clamping it securely to the workbench, and place the drill-bit into the hole, resuming the cutting from the opposite side. The circular saw-cuts will meet midway through the material, leaving a perfectly rounded edge.

Cut a second disc of the same 50mm (2in) diameter, then remove the cylindrical blade from the circular plate, replacing it with a smaller blade of approximately 28mm (1⅛in) diameter. Using the same technique, cut six discs to this size.

Each disc, of course, has a hole bored right through at the centre, equal to the diameter of the saw's pilot bit, and the next task is to plug these holes with matching dowel material. However, cut the dowels to a length of 16mm (⅝in), so that they do not pass fully through the thickness of the wheels, leaving a 3mm (⅛in)-deep impression in the middle when viewed from the outer surface. Mix some wood glue, brush it into the holes and on to the dowels and tap them gently into the wheels.

When the glue has dried, mark the centre of each dowel where it lies flush with the wheel on the inner surface, and drill down at this point with a 2mm (3⁄32in)-diameter twist drill to a depth of 9mm (⅜in), ready to receive the steel axle rod, which will later be cut from 2mm (3⁄32in)-diameter material.

Rub down each wheel with fine-grade sandpaper to remove any traces of glue, and give two coats of black gloss paint.

THE TRACTOR

Mark out the shape of the tractor on to a piece of wood, and cut it out with the coping saw or jig-saw. Mark in the positions of the front and back axles, first measuring them on the one side, then squaring across the bottom edge and repeating the measuring and marking in corresponding positions on the opposite side.

Clamp the piece of wood firmly at the side of the workbench, then fit a 2mm (3⁄32in)-diameter twist drill in the handbrace and carefully bore down in each of the marked axle positions. Be sure to keep the drill held perpendicularly to the surface of the wood, and when the bit has passed halfway down through the thickness of the tractor, stop drilling and turn the piece over, repeating the same process. If you have measured and marked correctly, and drilled accurately, the holes should meet up within the wood.

The rear end of the tractor is chamfered on both sides. The two areas of waste

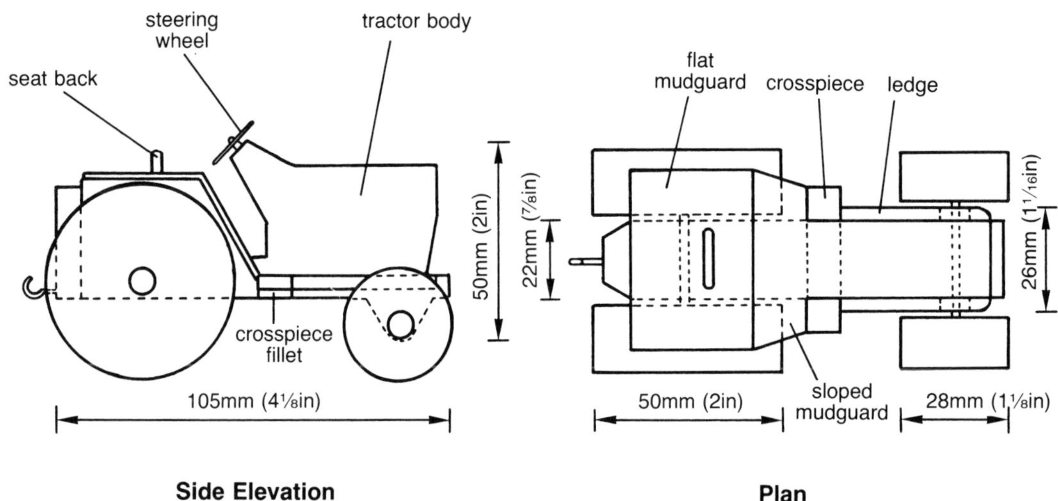

Main dimensions of the tractor.

After the body of the tractor has been marked out and cut to shape, the wheel axle positions are measured and drilled through the block from both sides, thus ensuring that the wood does not splinter on the under-surface.

should be marked in clearly before any attempt is made to remove the unwanted corners. First, make certain that the end-grain is cut perfectly square. Then take the mortise gauge and set the gap between the spurs so that it is equal to one-third the thickness of the wood. Adjust the position of the fence so that the two spurs are placed centrally across the thickness – this can be checked by holding the gauge first from one side and then from the other: if the pin-point holes made by the spurs coincide, they are correctly centred.

Scribe a pair of parallel lines down the end-grain from top edge to bottom edge with the mortise gauge.

Now slacken off the screw that tightens the fence to the stock of the gauge, and push it right up against the closer of the two spurs. Re-tighten the screw and then, using the mortise gauge effectively as a marking gauge, scribe a single line down both sides of the piece, bearing the fence along the end-grain. The limits of the chamfer have now been clearly marked.

Probably the best way of removing the unwanted corners is to clamp the piece firmly flat on the workbench again, and chop away most of the waste with a wide-bladed chisel and mallet. As you approach the marked lines, the remainder can either be pared away with the same chisel, or planed off with the smoothing plane.

The next stage is to mark out and cut the housing slot in the bottom edge of the tractor to receive the crosspiece that projects outwards on both sides in imitation of a step and footrest for the tractor driver. This will be prepared from two lollypop sticks, each of which measure approximately 9mm (3⁄8in) wide by 2mm (3⁄32in) thick.

The housing slot is cut in a similar manner to that of a housing joint. Its position is not absolutely critical, and can be determined from the position indicated in the diagram. The two ends of the slot should be set 9mm (3⁄8in) apart, and gauged to a depth of 6mm (1⁄4in).

Clamp the tractor upside-down in the vice, and cut down both ends with the tenon saw or hacksaw, working the blade on the waste side of each line, and stop cutting when the saw just touches the depth-line. Chop out the waste with a 9mm (3⁄8in) chisel, working the blade first from one side and then from the other. Trim the slot so that the edges are square.

The length of the slot may be checked easily with a lollypop stick. This project actually requires quite a lot, so if you have a particular aversion to lollypops, you will have to prepare your own strips

Mark and cut out the housing slot in the bottom edge of the tractor, and then prepare the crosspiece and fillet which are glued within it.

of 9×2mm (3⁄8×3⁄32in) hardwood, fitting the stick into the gap. If any resistance is felt, pare away more wood from the ends of the slot until the stick slides in easily.

Cut two sticks to a length of 40mm (19⁄16in) each, then glue them together, one on top of the other, and fit the assembly into the slot so that 9mm (3⁄8in) projects on either side. As their combined thickness will equal 4mm (3⁄16in) in what is a 6mm (1⁄4in) deep slot, a shallow recess of 2mm (3⁄32in) remains, and this is taken up with a crosspiece fillet cut to a length of 22mm (7⁄8in) using another section of lollypop stick. Wipe away all traces of glue from the joining surfaces.

The ledges are fitted in front of the crosspiece, just butting up against its forward edge on both sides, and stopping 6mm (1⁄4in) short of the front of the trac-

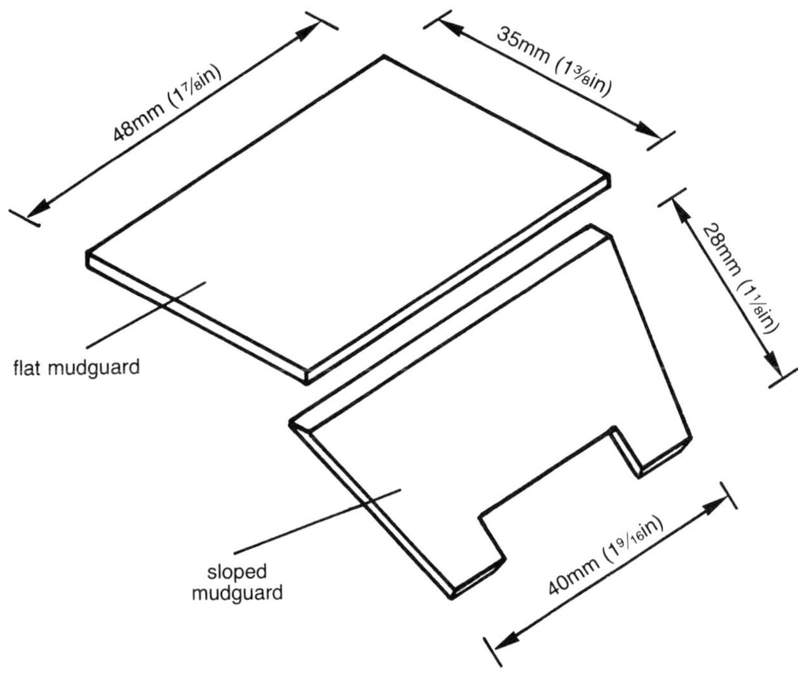

Dimensions and method of assembly for the flat mudguard and sloped mudguard of the tractor.

tor. Once again, these are made from two strips of lollypop stick, glued together, and cut to dimensions of 35×4×2mm (1⅜×3/16×3/32in). As lollypop sticks have rounded ends, it is simple to arrange for the double strips to be cut from each end, and to use the rounding off to provide the desired curve at the front corner of each ledge. Glue the two strips together first, and when the glue had dried thoroughly, rub down the edges and glue the assemblies to the sides of the tractor.

Cut the mudguards to size from 3mm (⅛in) thick birch-faced plywood. These are made in two parts: the first is a plain rectangle glued in place across the top edge, whilst the second is mounted at an angle, and has a piece cut away at the bottom so that it reaches down to the crosspiece and just touches the rear top corner. It is cut in the form of a trapezium, in such a way that the upper edge is equal to the width of the mudguard fixed to the top edge, whilst the lower edge is equal to the 40mm (1⅜in) length of the crosspiece.

When both parts of the mudguards are firmly attached and the glue has dried thoroughly, rub them down with medium-grade and then fine-grade sandpaper to round off the edges and corners. Indeed, all the main corners of the tractor should be similarly sandpapered to produce a smooth finish.

A steering wheel may be cut out from a

piece of thin plywood and attached to the tractor with 3mm (1/8in)-diameter dowelling, and a short length of 6×4mm (1/4×3/16in) wood strip glued to the upper mudguard to form a seat-back for the driver.

Paint the tractor in a colour scheme of your own choice – this one is painted blue and white.

Cut two pieces of 2mm (3/32in)-diameter steel axle rod to length, and fit the wheels. Note that the two back wheels can be fitted straight on, but the two front wheels will require small spacer blocks so that they do not rub against the projecting ledge on each side of the tractor. These spacer blocks are made from short lengths of 9mm (3/8in)-diameter dowelling, which have 2mm (3/32in)-diameter holes drilled through them. A small amount of adhesive should be used to bond the axles to the wheels.

Lastly, a small stainless steel hook is screwed into the back of the tractor and is secured with adhesive.

THE CART

The cart towed behind the tractor is of the open type, with slatted sides and solid front and back panels assembled on to a base. The base consists of a floor panel for the cart, attached to a solid block below that carries the wheels.

Measure and mark the wheel block on a solid piece of wood measuring 90×22×22mm (3½×7/8×7/8in). At a point 13mm (½in) from each end, on the bottom edge, draw in two curved projections through which 2mm (3/32in)-diameter holes are drilled to receive the axle rods, similar to those made at the front of the tractor, except that these for the cart are

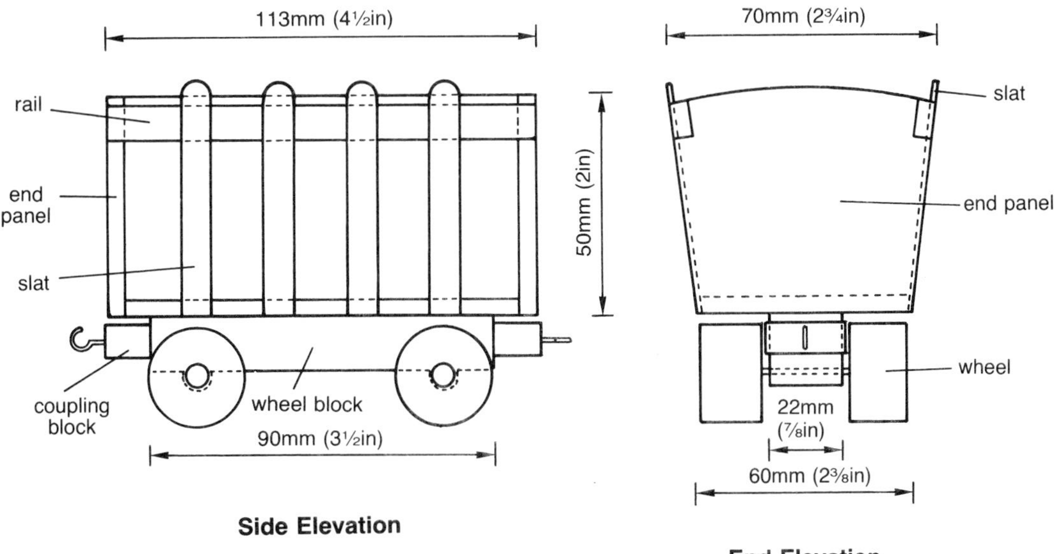

Main dimensions of the cart.

Mark the top edges of the end panels with a pair of compasses to give a gentle curve. Note that the point of the compasses is positioned on a piece of scrap wood with a straight line running at right-angles to the bottom edge of the panel, centrally placed.

less pronounced, projecting only by 6mm (¼in) or so. Cut the block to shape using the coping saw or jig-saw, trimming the ends perfectly square.

Cut the floor panel to size from a piece of 6mm (¼in) thick oak measuring 100×60mm (4×2⅜in). Cut the two end panels from material of the same thickness, noting that the sides are splayed outwards in typical farm-cart fashion. The top edges are curved slightly upwards.

The slatted sides are made very simply by keying a top rail between the front and back panel, and attaching a row of lollypop sticks, cut in half, to the rail and the edge of the floor panel, both of which are notched in suitable places to receive them. Start by working out the positions of the lollypop sticks along both sides of the floor panel, and mark in the notches, cutting them out with the hacksaw and chisel. The depth of each notch should be the same as the thickness of the stick. Take two lengths of 9×6mm (⅜×¼in) material for the rails and notch these correspondingly. Both rails are cut longer than is necessary and will be trimmed later.

Measure and mark in the positions of two notches in each of the end panels to receive the rails, these being cut similarly with the hacksaw and 6mm (¼in) chisel.

Gather together four washed and dried lollypop sticks and cut them all in half.

Mix a small amount of wood glue and apply it by brush to the ends of the floor panel, to the corresponding abutting ends of the front and back panels, to the notches cut in the front and back panels and to the rails. Assemble the cart, pressing the butt joints firmly together, and

Cut the notches in the sides of the floor panel by sawing at each end of the marked positions with the hacksaw and paring away the waste with a thin chisel. The depth of each notch should be equal to the thickness of the cart slats.

adjusting the position of both rails so that their notches occur directly above the notches cut in the floor panel. Apply a little glue to the notches and fit the halved lollypop sticks to make the slats. Finally, clamp the assembly together to hold the butt joints in contact while the glue sets hard.

The butt joints between the front and back panels and the floor panel may be strengthened by drilling 2mm (3/32in)-diameter holes into the joints and inserting lengths of glued 2mm (3/32in) dowelling.

When the glue is completely dry, trim the ends of the two rails so that they are flush with the outer surfaces of the front and back panels.

Mount the notched rails into notches cut at the top corners of the end panels, setting them so that the slats can be attached in an upright manner.

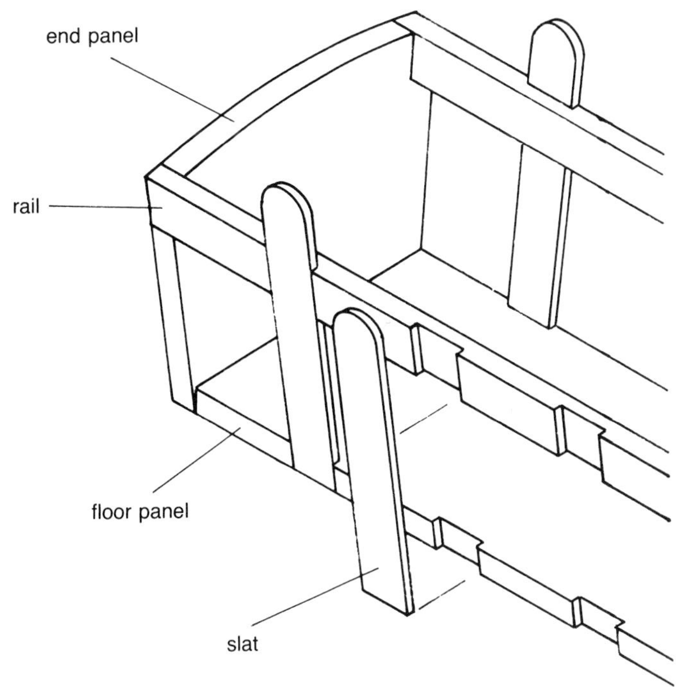

Assembling the slats to the floor panel and rail of the cart.

The axle holes may be enlarged with a twist drill if there is a tendency for the axles to bind. The cart is firmly clamped in the vice, and the drill bit carefully turned in the original holes.

Mix more glue and fix the cart assembly on to the wheel block, cut two small blocks from 13×9mm (½×⅜in) ramin, both measuring 25mm (1in) in length. Glue these to the two ends of the block as attachment points for the screw-eye at one end, which fastens to the hook of the tractor, and a hook at the other end to couple up any additional carts.

Paint the cart in a suitable green or brown paint, and attach the wheels.

Cutting List

THE TRACTOR

Tractor body: one of 105×50×22mm (4⅛×2×⅞in)
Crosspiece: two of 40×9×2mm (1⁹⁄₁₆×⅜×³⁄₃₂in)
Crosspiece fillet: one of 22×9×2mm (⅞×⅜×³⁄₃₂in)
Ledge: four of 35×4×2mm (1⅜×³⁄₁₆×³⁄₃₂in)
Flat mudguard: one of 48×35×3mm (1⅞×1⅜×⅛in)
Sloped mudguard: one of 48×28×3mm (1⅞×1⅛×⅛in)
Front wheel: two of 19×28mm (¾×1⅛in) diameter
Back wheel: two of 19×50mm (¾×2in) diameter
Seat-back: one of 16×6×4mm (⅝×¼×³⁄₁₆in)
Steering wheel: one of 2×16mm (³⁄₃₂×⅝in) diameter

THE CART

Wheel block: one of 90×22×22mm (3½×⅞×⅞in)
Floor panel: one of 100×60×6mm (4×2⅜×¼in)
End panel: two of 70×50×6mm (2¾×2×¼in)
Rail: two of 112×9×6mm (4⅜×⅜×¼in)
Slat: eight of 50×9×2mm (2×⅜×³⁄₃₂in)
Coupling block: two of 25×13×9mm (1×½×⅜in)
Wheel: four of 19×28mm (¾×1⅛in) diameter

CHAPTER THIRTEEN

THE TOBOGGAN

The child's toboggan, or sledge, provides an exciting way of sliding down a slope, whether on snow or slippery grass. In its simplest form, it is no more than a flat wooden board mounted on a pair of runners. It must be sturdy enough in construction to withstand rough use.

The choice of wood needs some consideration: for greatest strength and durability, a hardwood will undoubtedly yield the best material, at the expense of weight. If a young child is to tow it uphill, it must not be too heavy or it will prove unmanageable, in which case lighter softwood would seem better.

The toboggan illustrated is built from ordinary redwood, or deal, and you will have to make a special point of asking the supplier to pick out lengths that are as free of knots as possible. Fortunately, all the sections are fairly limited in size, so it should not be too difficult for the woodyard to find appropriate lengths.

If you have a lot of left-over pieces from other work, sapele or utile would be good hardwood alternatives.

Start by measuring and marking the two runners to size. They are each rounded off at the front end, and sloped at the back. Being identical, the pro-

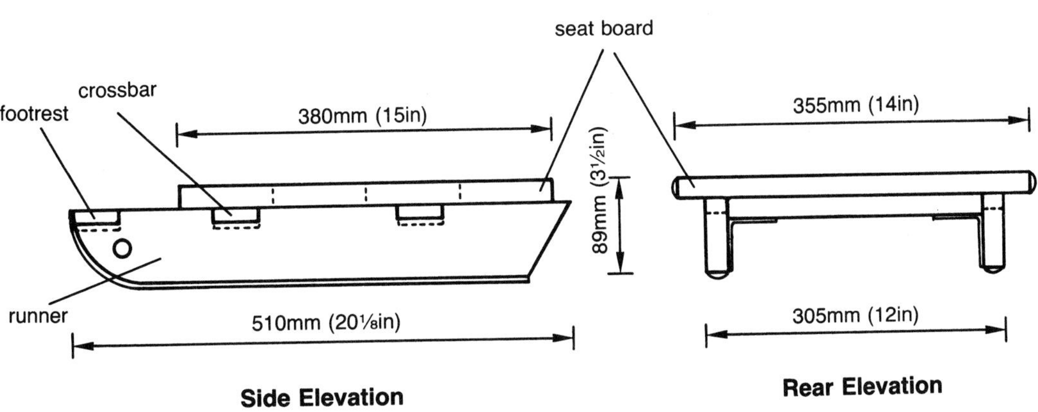

Main dimensions of the toboggan.

cedure is the same. Take a piece of 70× 19mm (2¾×¾in) material and mark it to an overall length of 510mm (20in), squaring all around at both ends. Decide which end is to be the front of the runner and which is to be the back.

At the front, measure a distance 70mm (2¾in) back from the squared line, and square this off also. Taking a pair of geometrical compasses, set them to a radius of 70mm (2¾in), place the point on this second line, 2mm (3⁄32in) down from the top edge of the wood, and describe an arc between the bottom edge and the squared line denoting the end of the piece. Cut along this curved line with the jig-saw or coping saw to give the rounded front end.

At the back, measure a distance 40mm (1 9⁄16in) forward from the squared line, squaring this off in a similar way. Draw a straight line from the bottom edge of the wood that coincides with this line, to the top edge of the squared line that denotes the end of the piece. Cut along this sloped line with the tenon saw, removing the waste and thus completing the cutting to shape of the runner.

Measure and mark the two crossbars to size. They are cut from 45×19mm (1¾× ¾in) material, each measuring 305mm (12in) in length. They are lap-jointed to the top edge of the runners, and these joints are additionally reinforced by mounting L-shaped metal brackets between the underside of the crossbars and

Cut away the waste from the curved front end of the runner with the jig-saw.

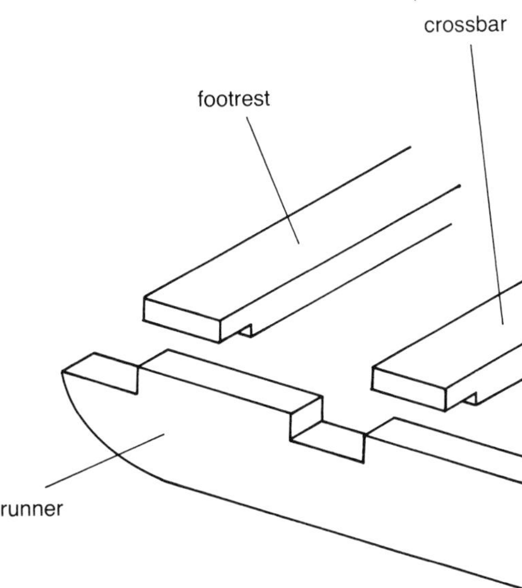

Exploded lapped joints between the runner, and one crossbar and the footrest.

the inside surfaces of the runners. Lap joints are chosen in preference to halved joints, because the laps only require a small amount of waste to be removed from the crossbars, whereas halved joints would reduce their thickness by half and, consequently, weaken them.

The dimensions of the lap call for notches to be cut to a depth of 16mm (5⁄8in) in the top edge of the runners, and a shoulder to be cut to a depth of 3mm (1⁄8in) across the thickness of the crossbars. First measure and mark in the positions of the notches to be cut in both runners: the front crossbar is set back 150mm (5 7⁄8in) from the front end, and the back crossbar is set forward by 150mm (5 7⁄8in) from the back end. Each notch is 45mm (1 3⁄4in) wide, equal to the width of the crossbar material, and

Measure and mark in the positions of the lapped joints on the top edge of the runners, using a tape measure, square and pencil.

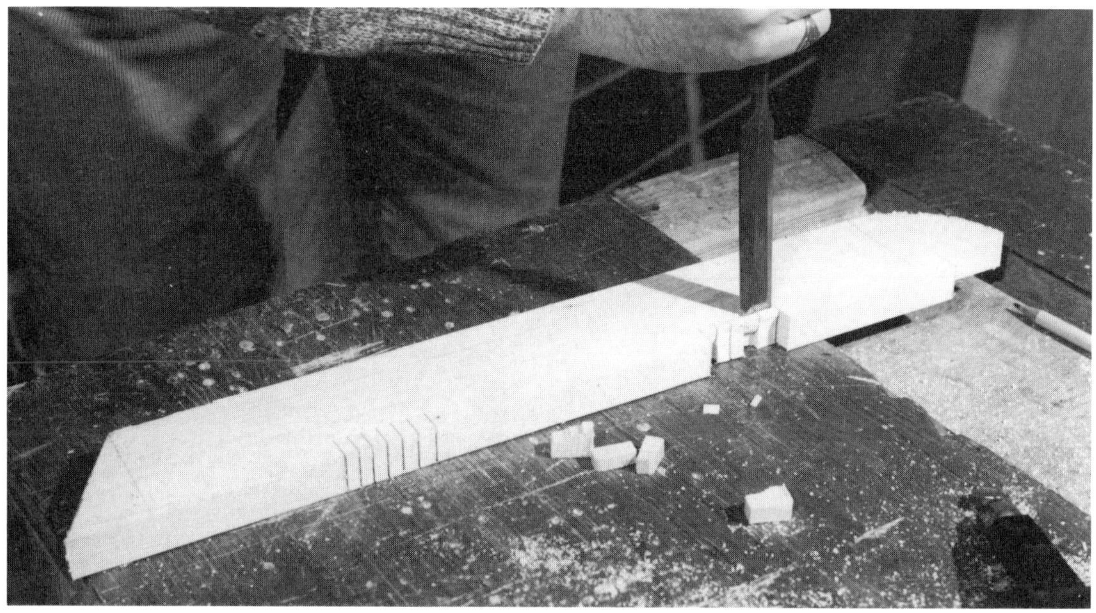

Chop away the waste from the lapped joints on the top edge of the runner, using a wide-bladed chisel and mallet.

16mm (⅝in) deep. Mark in the notches with the square and pencil.

Taking the runners in turn, mount them in the workbench vice, and cut down the sides of the marked out areas as far as the depth line, using the tenon saw. Remove the runner from the vice, lay it flat on the workbench, and chop out the waste with a chisel and mallet, making the cuts with the chisel firstly from one side of the runner and then from the other.

Measure and mark the corresponding shoulders, one at each end of the two crossbars. Start by measuring a point 19mm (¾in) from the end-grain, and squaring across the one side and two edges of the crossbar. Then set the marking gauge so that the distance between the fence and the spur is 16mm (⅝in), equal to the depth of each notch in the runners, and scribe a line along the two edges and end-grain at both ends of the two crossbars. Remove the waste with the tenon saw and make a test fitting of the four lap joints.

The footrest that is attached between the two runners at the front end of the toboggan is of the same cross-sectional dimensions as the crossbars, and this also is lap-jointed in position. Indeed, the method of jointing is almost identical to that used for the crossbars, except that, instead of a notch being cut along the length of the top edge, it is cut right at the front end, so that the waste is removed by making two cuts with the tenon saw. The two ends of the footrest are similarly given 3mm (⅛in)-deep shoulders.

Where the two crossbars are glued in position and then reinforced with L-shaped steel brackets, the footrest at the front is glued and screwed in place. Drill

Assemble the crossbars to the runners with glue, and strengthen with L-shaped steel brackets.

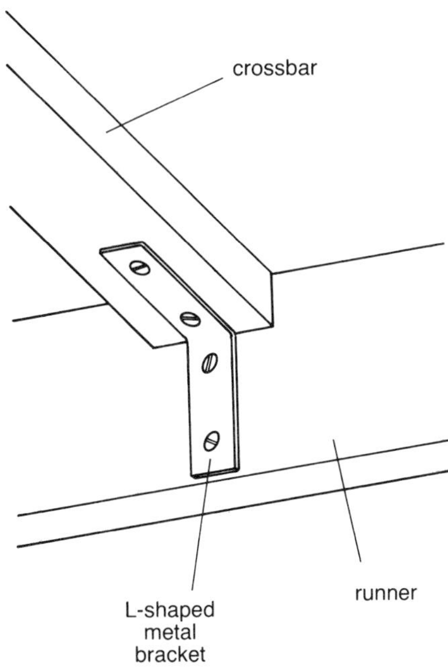

Right-angled bracket strengthens the lapped joints between the runners and crossbars.

Once the crossbars are in place, fit the footrest at the front, adding woodscrews for additional strength.

out one hole per joint to a depth of 25mm (1in) using a number 8 drill bit, countersinking on the upper surface of the footrest. Fit the 50×50mm (2×2in) L-shaped brackets in position between the crossbar and the runners and mark in the screw-holes, drilling each hole to a depth of 13mm (½in).

Mix a quantity of wood glue and apply it to all the lap joints, then tap the crossbars into their notches and fit the L-shaped brackets with 13mm (½in) number 10 woodscrews; place the footrest in its rebate and fix it down with 25mm (1in) number 8 woodscrews. Set the assembly to one side for a day or so while the glue hardens completely.

The seat boards are made up of four 355mm (14in)-long pieces of 95×19mm (3¾×¾in) material, all butt-jointed edge to edge. Begin by cutting them equally to length and planing the ends square. In addition to gluing the boards on to the top edges of the runners, they are screwed in place, using 50mm (2in) number 8 woodscrews. The seat boards overhang the runners by 25mm (1in) on either side. Making allowance for this, measure and mark in two screw-hole positions at both ends of each board, bore them out with a number 8 drill-bit and countersink.

Place the boards in position on the runners, butting them up tightly against one another, and leaving a gap of 25mm (1in) between the back edge of the rearmost board and the ends of the runners, and mark the screw-holes on the top edges of the runners using a bradawl. Drill the holes to a depth of 30mm (1$^{3}/_{16}$in).

Mix more wood glue, apply it to the

Glue and screw the seat boards on to the runners.

Plane across the end-grain of the assembled seat boards so that they are square and level.

Cut a piece of seat edging strip to length and glue it in position, securing it with several panel pins.

Drill a hole for the towing rope near the front end of each runner. A block of scrap wood is clamped beneath the hole to avoid splintering the inside surface of the runner.

edges of the seat boards and the top edges of the runners and fit the four boards in place, screwing them fully home.

Cut two 380mm (15in) lengths of rounded hardwood edging strip and glue them to the sides of the seat, covering the exposed end-grain of the four seat boards. Tack them down with panel pins.

The same edging strip material may be attached to the bottom edge of the runners, for improved contact with the ground. Note that the strip will have to be bent to follow the upward curve at the front end of each runner. The wood can be made much more flexible if it is thoroughly soaked in water or subjected to a jet of steam from a boiling kettle. Bend the wood gradually to shape. It is probably best to cut each strip rather on the long side – the surplus can easily be trimmed later. Tack it on to the edge of the runner with panel pins, to hold it in position whilst the wood dries. Do not drive the panel pins fully home, as they will have to be pulled out later with the pliers.

When the edging strip has dried, it should retain some of its curved attitude. Remove the panel pins, mix some wood glue and apply this thoroughly to both joining surfaces, placing the strip back in position and tapping the panel pins back into their holes until they are flush with the surface. When the glue has dried and set hard, cut the overhanging pieces of edging strip from the front and back of the runners.

Drill two 13mm (½in)-diameter holes, one per runner, near to the front end to receive a length of rope that is used for towing the toboggan along the ground. Pass the rope through each hole and tie a knot on the inside to hold it in place. Arrange the length of the rope to be such that it can be stored by passing it around the back of the seat, where there is just sufficient tension to hold it in place. This is where it should be kept when the toboggan is in use.

FINISHING TOUCHES

Treat all surfaces of the toboggan with an exterior-type wood finish – the sort that usually contains a dye – applying several coats to make certain that the wood is well protected against the damp. Finally, before venturing on to the slopes, give the runners a good polish to make them slide easily.

Cutting List

Runner: two of 510×70×19mm (20⅛×2¾×¾in)
Crossbar: two of 305×45×19mm (12×1¾×¾in)
Footrest: one of 305×45×19mm (12×1¾×¾in)
Seat board: four of 355×95×19mm (14×3¾×¾in)
Seat edging: two of 380×19mm (15×¾in) rounded strip
Runner edging: two of 550×19mm (21⅝×¾in) rounded strip

Chapter Fourteen

The Windmill Money Box

Money boxes come in all shapes and sizes. This example is designed in the form of an old- fashioned windmill, typical of the sort that can be found dotted around the low-lying countryside of East Anglia. The main feature of this small model is that the sails turn round when money is dropped through the slot in the top.

The windmill is constructed in two parts, which fit easily together. The main part consists of the round tower, which is a hollow tapered wooden cylinder into which the money drops and is stored; the second part is the detachable domed top with the four sails, the connecting shaft and the simple four-bladed paddle that operates the turning of the sails as coins drop through the slot in the top and fall on to it.

Two other features add a touch of authenticity to the windmill, although they are not intended to be an exact copy of the real thing. These are the wooden gantry, or walkway, that runs around the tower, level with the lowest point of the sails' rotation; and the fantail at the rear of the top, which in the full-sized windmill has a special gear mechanism to turn the top and thus automatically keep the sails square to the wind, regardless of the direction from which it blows.

In this instance, the fantail is merely included for the sake of appearance and, of course, has no control over the position of the top. Small window openings and a doorway may either be cut right through the wall of the tower, engraved on the surface or painted on.

Although the details of the windmill are essentially quite simple and straightforward, the various stages involved in its construction are actually rather complicated, calling for a high degree of skill and access to a woodturning lathe, or, at the very least, a lathe attachment powered by an electric drill. This is really unavoidable if the tower and the top are to have a perfectly smooth finish. However, if you do not have the opportunity to use a lathe, but are prepared to exercise plenty of patience, a worthwhile result will be achieved using a chisel, spokeshave and sandpaper.

THE TOWER

Begin by making the tower. As you will see, this is made up of nine segments or rings. Starting with the base at the bottom – this is a solid disc of wood referred to as the first ring – then moving upwards, each of the remaining eight rings have a circle cut out from the centre. For the purpose of construction a

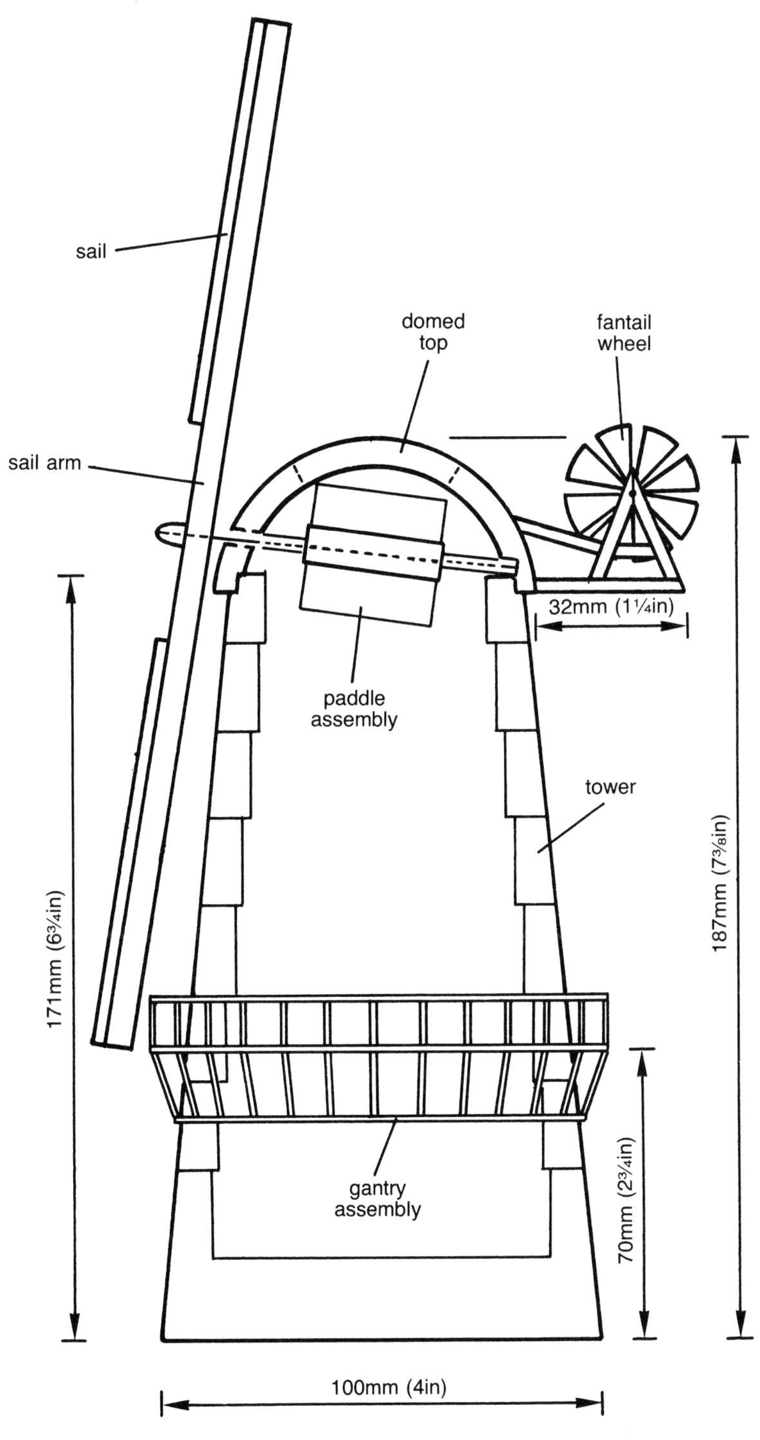

Side view of windmill.

tenth segment is added at the top but this, like the base, is a solid disc. Each segment measures 19mm thick.

The wood used in this example is sapele, or utile, which responds favourably to woodturning. It has a fine grain structure and should be free of awkward knots. The dark reddish-brown of the wood does not matter, because the windmill ought to be painted.

Make sure that you have enough of the material to be able to cut ten rings. Clearly, as the tower is tapered, the rings will have a smaller diameter the higher up they go. The first and the tenth ring only have an outer diameter, because they are solid discs, but all the others have an inner diameter also, indicating the size of the circle that needs to be cut out.

The first ring and the tenth ring have outer diameters of 100mm (4in) and 64mm ($2\frac{1}{2}$in) respectively. The second ring has an outer/inner diameter of 96mm/74mm ($3\frac{3}{4}\times2\frac{7}{8}$in); the third ring is 92mm/70mm ($3\frac{5}{8}\times2\frac{3}{4}$in); the fourth ring is 88mm/66mm ($3\frac{1}{4}\times2\frac{5}{8}$in); the fifth ring is 84mm/62mm ($3\frac{5}{16}\times2\frac{7}{16}$in); the sixth ring is 80mm/58mm($3\frac{1}{8}\times2\frac{1}{4}$in); the seventh ring is 76mm/54mm ($3\times2\frac{1}{8}$in); the eighth ring is 72mm/50mm ($2\frac{13}{16}\times$ 2in); and the ninth ring is 68mm/46mm ($2\frac{11}{16}\times1\frac{13}{16}$in).

Using a pair of geometrical compasses, mark out all ten rings on the wood, which must be completely flat and smooth. Remember that the figures just quoted for the rings are diameters, so all of these must be halved to give the corresponding radii. As already stated, the two outermost rings are simply plain discs, having only one marked circle, but all the rest have inner and outer circles, each of which must now be cut out with great accuracy.

Mark the ten rings of the tower on to lengths of wood, using a pair of compasses.

Assuming that all of the circles are marked out on one or two large pieces of material, set as closely as possible to one another for economy, it is important to begin by cutting out the inner circles first, while the wood can still be clamped to the end of the workbench.

To remove the inner circle from any piece of wood, the best tool is either a jigsaw or coping saw, the jig-saw being preferable because it cuts quickly and is easier to steer accurately around a curved line. Whichever tool you decide to use, there is one essential preliminary step – a hole must be drilled through the wood, near to the marked line within the central area of waste. This hole is needed to admit the blade of the saw and it does not have to be of a particularly large diameter: 13mm ($\frac{1}{2}$in) is sufficient.

Cut out the inner circles of eight of the rings with the jig-saw, clamping the wood firmly at the end of the workbench.

Always drill the hole from both sides of the wood, first boring from one side until the tip of the bit just breaks through, and turning the piece over to complete the drilling from the opposite side, in order to avoid splintering the surface.

Insert the blade of the jig-saw or coping saw through the hole, and start cutting towards the inner line in a gradual curve, so that when the blade just makes contact with the circle, you can continue cutting around it in a single action of the saw. For the entire duration of the cut, make sure that the blade of the saw remains perpendicular to the surface of the wood – an especially important point when using the coping saw, which has a habit of wandering!

Having taken out the centres from eight of the circular pieces of wood, the next task is to cut around the outer lines to complete the preparation of the rings. At each end the first and tenth segments remain as solid discs.

Now the tower can be constructed. Commencing at the base, place the disc flat on the workbench with the marked side facing downwards. The reason for this is not because of the marked circle – this, after all, has been cut to the line anyway – but because the pin-point mark made by the pair of compasses is still visible at the centre of the disc, and must be clearly visible for later reference.

Mix a fairly large quantity of wood glue and apply it by brush on to the outer perimeter of the base and on the underside of the second ring. Bring the two pieces into contact, taking care to adjust the position of the upper ring so that it is

Glue the ten rings together, altering the grain direction of each successive ring to strengthen the structure.

placed centrally on the base. One tip to bear in mind is to locate it so that its grain is slightly different in orientation from the base, and to carry on in similar fashion so that the third ring is turned differently from the second, and so on. When the first two segments are satisfactorily assembled, apply glue to the upper surface of the second ring and the underside of the third ring, and continue building up the segments until finally the tenth ring – the second solid disc – is fitted on top with its pin-point compass mark on the upper face. Place a heavy weight on to the assembly to keep all the joining surfaces pressed together whilst the glue dries.

After a day or so, remove the weight and examine the assembly to check that all the segments are properly and securely joined – otherwise the whole lot could fly apart on the lathe. Probably glue will have squeezed out from the joints in various places and run into long blobs. These should be carefully scraped off with the chisel to present a column consisting of stepped sections.

To refine these steps into a single smooth surface, the column is mounted in the lathe. The pin-point marks left by the compasses at each end show where the headstock and tailstock must make contact. Set the lathe spinning and, with the eyes properly shielded from flying splinters by protective spectacles, run a spindle gouge along the length of the tower, gradually whittling away the raised steps and turning the segments into one continuous level surface. It should only be possible to distinguish

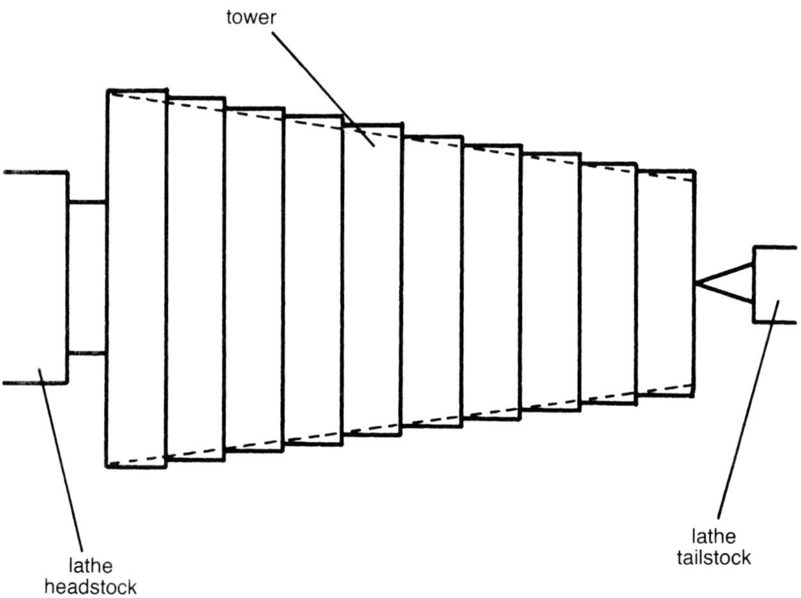

Mounting tower assembly in lathe for turning.

Mount the tower between centres in the lathe, and smooth the surface down with the spindle gouge and woodturning chisel.

one ring from the next by a barely discernible thin line, of a hair's breadth.

Now cut a rebate into the ninth ring at the point where it adjoins the tenth, to create the joint with the domed top. The tool used to cut the rebate is the parting tool. It should be cut to a width of 9mm (3⁄8in) and a depth of 3mm (1⁄8in). Finally, with the tower still turning in the lathe, apply a piece of medium-grade sandpaper to the surface to smooth out any small irregularities and finish off with fine-grade paper. Wear a glove so that your fingers do not get burnt, as the sandpaper can heat up very quickly with the friction.

Remove the tower from the lathe, lay it carefully on the workbench, cushioned in a cloth to protect the smooth finish, and separate the tenth ring from the rest of the column by cutting along the joint

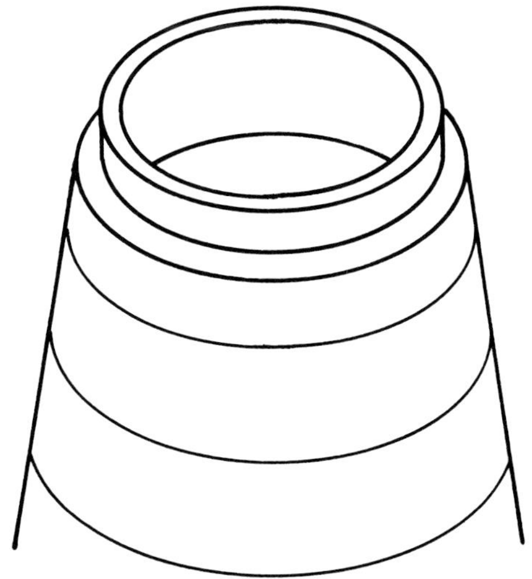

A rebate is cut at the top of the tower, in the ninth ring, to receive the rebated dome. Once the tenth ring is removed, the rebate can clearly be seen.

inside the rebate with the tenon saw. Now that the lid has been taken off the column, so to speak, the tapered cylinder of the tower is apparent, as indeed is the fact that the interior is still stepped and, therefore, rather rough. However, it would be extremely difficult to smooth out the inside of the tower and really rather wasteful of time and effort.

THE DOMED TOP

The next task is to make the domed top. Essentially this consists of turning a hemisphere twice – once from the outside and once from the inside, so that as far as possible the wood remains of uniform thickness. Start by taking a block of wood measuring 72×42mm (2¹³⁄₁₆×1⅝in), and mark a circle on one side with a pair of geometrical compasses whose radius has been set to 34mm (1¹¹⁄₃₂in). With a width of 72mm (2¹³⁄₁₆in), there should be 2mm (³⁄₃₂in) to spare between the circumference of the circle and each edge. Clamp the block at the side of the workbench and cut around the circle with the jig-saw or coping saw, keeping the blade on the waste side of the line throughout the entire cut. The result is a solid disc of wood measuring 42mm (1⅝in) thick.

This time, the block must be mounted on to the face-plate of the lathe, and the outer surface of the hemisphere worked using the spindle gouge. A simple checking mould can be made by marking out a semi-circle of 34mm (1¹¹⁄₃₂in) radius on to a piece of thin card and cutting away the inside portion. Stop the lathe frequently and check progress by fitting the mould over the turned block – when it fits perfectly you know that a hemisphere has

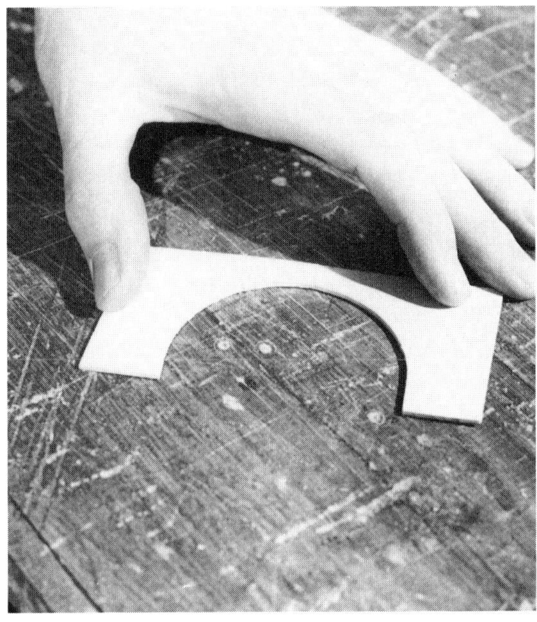

A card template has the curvature of the domed top cut in it, so that the outer contour of the dome can be checked as it is turned on the lathe.

A spindle gouge is used to work the outer contour of the dome.

been achieved. Actually, the dome will not be a true hemisphere because, whereas the radius of the circle is 34mm (1 11/32in), the thickness of the wood is 42mm (1 5/8in), so the base of the dome is cylindrical for 8mm (11/32in). There is, of course, a reason for this.

Removing the solid dome from the face-plate of the lathe, it must now be apparent that the wood needs to be mounted the opposite way around in order to cut out the inside of the hemisphere. But how is the piece to be attached to the face-plate? If you have access to a proper workshop lathe, the jaws of the chuck may be opened sufficiently to clamp the wood in position, and you simply proceed as normal with the removal of the waste. But a flat face-plate presents something of a problem.

The solution is to make an outer casing, into which the dome can be fitted. The method may sound complicated but, in fact, it is most straightforward.

Take a block of wood measuring at least 100mm (4in) wide and 50mm (2in) thick, and mark two concentric circles on one side – that is to say, circles that have the same centre. The outer circles should be of 50mm (2in) radius, and the inner one is exactly equal to the radius of the hemispherical dome – in other words, 34mm (1 11/32in). If anything, make the inner circle slightly too small because it can always be enlarged. Cut around both circular lines to leave a wooden ring.

Check that the dome fits tightly into the inner part of the ring, and assemble it in place with wood glue, applying the glue to the outer 6mm (1/4in) edge of the cylinder that projects beyond the dome. Tap it into the ring so that the flat end of the wood is flush with the outer face of the surrounding ring.

Taking a second piece of scrap wood, measuring at least 100mm (4in) wide and 25mm (1in) thick, mark a single circle of 50mm (2in) radius and cut it out with the saw, then glue this to the inner face of the ring, clamping the two parts firmly together until the glue has set hard. Making sure that the centre of this backing disc is in perfect alignment with the centre of the dome, mount the disc on to the faceplate of the lathe.

Set the lathe running, and carefully manipulate the spindle gouge to remove all the necessary waste from within the dome, measuring regularly to check that the thickness of the wood does not fall below 4mm (3/16in). A rebate must be worked on the inside edge to match that cut at the top of the tower; this can only

The second stage of preparation of the dome – the workpiece is being glued into a special sandwich of scrap wood, and the woodturning chisel is being manipulated through one scrap piece to hollow out the inside of the dome.

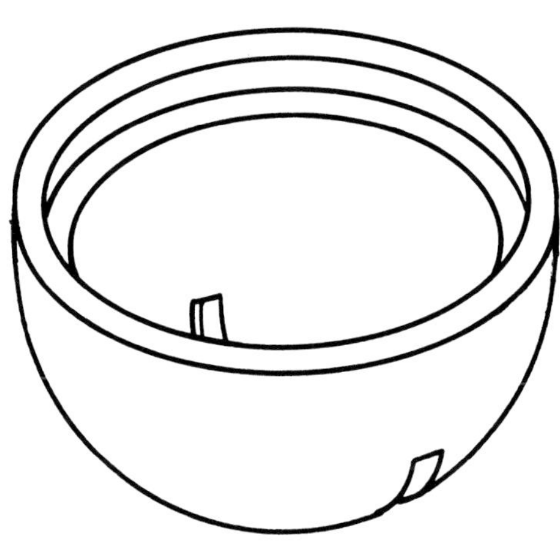

The rim of the dome is rebated, to fit the rebate at the top of the tower.

Cut a strip of paper or card and gum it in position on top of the dome before marking around it in pencil to delineate the money slot.

be carried out successfully by measuring the exact diameter and depth of the tower rebate, and transferring these measurements on to the dome rebate. It is better to err on the side of caution and take off too little waste, because the rebates can always be enlarged later by hand until one part slides tightly into the other.

Remember also, when cutting the rebate in the dome, that there is an excess of wood at the bottom, where it presently forms a cylinder, of which 6mm (¼in) is glued to the support ring. This 6mm surplus will be cut away with the parting tool as the last stage of the turning, giving a dome height of 36mm (1$^{7}/_{16}$in). By cutting into the base of the dome, you will actually weaken the glued joint sufficiently for the dome to be detached from the ring. Rub it down with sandpaper to round off the bottom edge, and press the dome into place on top of the tower.

Mark the slot for the coins on top of the dome. The slot should be just large

Drill a series of holes along the marked area with a narrow auger bit and, after sawing out the waste, trim the sides and ends of the slot with a sharp knife before filing smooth.

enough to accept the largest size of coin. The simplest way of marking it out is to cut a rectangle of thin card measuring 45x5mm (1¾x7/32in), apply some paper gum to one side of the card, and stick it down on the top of the dome, right in the middle. Mark around the four edges of the card in pencil, then peel it off. Drill a series of 4mm (3/16in)-diameter holes along the length of the marked area with a sharp twist drill, completing the removal of the waste with the coping saw and a flat file.

The Sails

The sails are made by first cutting two pieces of 6×6mm (¼×¼in) hardwood strip, each measuring 220mm (8⅝in) in length, and half-jointing them at the centre so that they form a cross. Through the middle of the halved joint, drill a 2mm (3/32in)-diameter hole with a small twist drill, to receive the axle shaft that will be cut from a length of 2mm(3/32in)-diameter steel axle material.

The four sail panels are constructed in

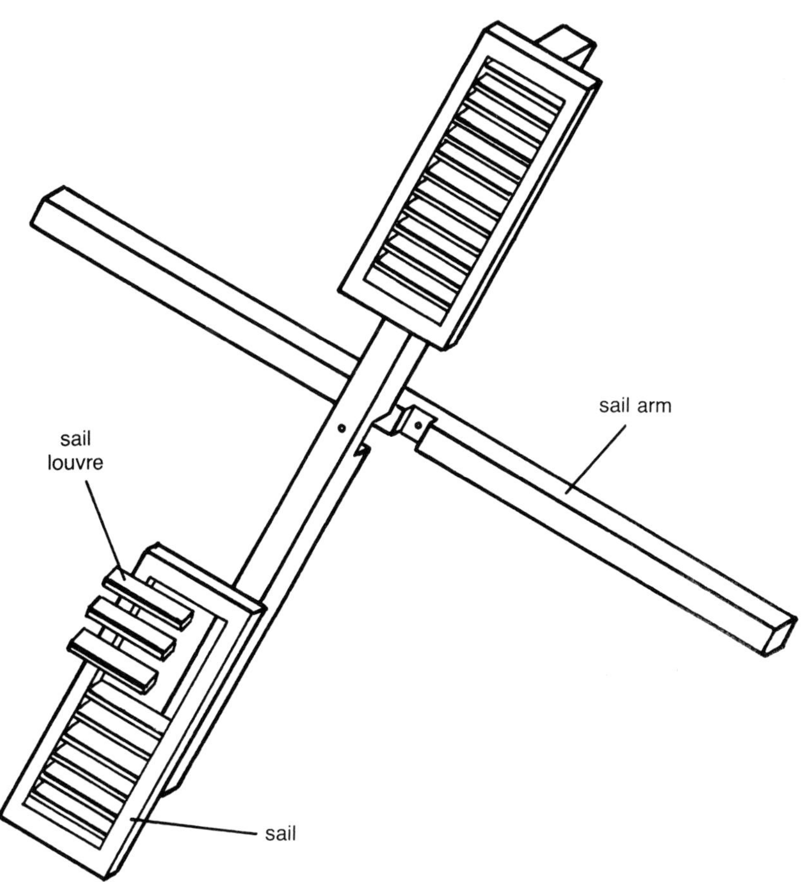

Exploded view of windmill sails.

Cut halved joints at the centre of each sail arm, and glue them together.

Mark the sails on thin plywood, and cut out the rectangular waste portions with a sharp knife, taking great care not to split the material.

the form of rectangular frames, with louvred strips slotted in between. The frames each measure 90×25mm (3⁹⁄₁₆× 1in), and are cut with a sharp knife from a piece of 3mm (⅛in)-thick birch-faced plywood. A smaller rectangle, measuring 84×19mm (3⁵⁄₁₆×¾in), is marked and cut out of the centre. A series of thin plywood strips, measuring 19×5mm (¾×⁷⁄₃₂in), are glued into the middle, each one set at a shallow angle. It is probably best to decide for yourself how many louvres you want, and whether to leave a few gaps here and there to suggest missing slats.

When the four sails are complete, glue them on to the wooden cross in such a way that each one lies flush with the end of the cross, and that they are all located centrally on the long arms.

Cut small pieces of wood to fit the sails in a louvred pattern, and glue them into place.

The Axle

Measure and mark in the positions of the two holes in the dome where the axle is to be fitted. Note that the line of the axle runs in precisely the same direction as that of the money slot. The front axle hole passes right through the dome, but the rear hole is stopped, being drilled to a depth of 2–3mm (3⁄32–1⁄8in). The holes are located in such a manner that the axle is angled upwards at approximately 10 degrees to the horizontal, in accordance with the usual design of windmills. Drill the holes with a 2mm (3⁄32in)-diameter twist drill. As the stopped hole is slightly inaccessible, you will probably have to work the drill-bit backwards and forwards by hand.

Cut a piece of 2mm (3⁄32in)-diameter steel axle rod so that it is long enough to rest inside the stopped hole and pass out through the front hole with 13mm (1⁄2in) to spare. Mark it off at this point and cut it to the required length with the hacksaw. Fit the sails in place. Prepare a rounded tip to fit over the projecting 6mm of axle. This tip is cut from 6mm (1⁄4in)-diameter dowelling, having first drilled a 2mm (3⁄32in)-diameter hole 6mm (1⁄4in) down into one end before cutting it to 10mm (13⁄32in) and rounding off the opposite end.

Mix a very small amount of strong epoxy resin adhesive and apply it to the projecting end of the axle shaft and to the hole bored into the tip. Apply a little adhesive also to the joining surfaces between the tip and the sails, and then press the tip on to the axle until it makes contact with the sail arms. Set to one side for several hours while the adhesive dries thoroughly. The sails are now bonded to the axle.

The Paddles

The paddle arrangement fits on the inside of the domed top and turns the sails when money is dropped through the slot.

First measure a piece of 9mm (3⁄8in)-diameter dowelling to a length of 30mm (13⁄16in), and cut it to size, making sure that the ends are perfectly square. Measure and mark in the exact centre of each end, and carefully drill a hole through the middle of the dowel using a 2mm (3⁄32in)-diameter twist drill, boring from one end and then from the other so that the holes meet halfway along its length.

The position of the four paddle vanes are now marked on the dowelling. The positions on the dowel end-grain correspond to three, six, nine and twelve o'clock. Make a small pencil mark in four places around its circumference, then lay

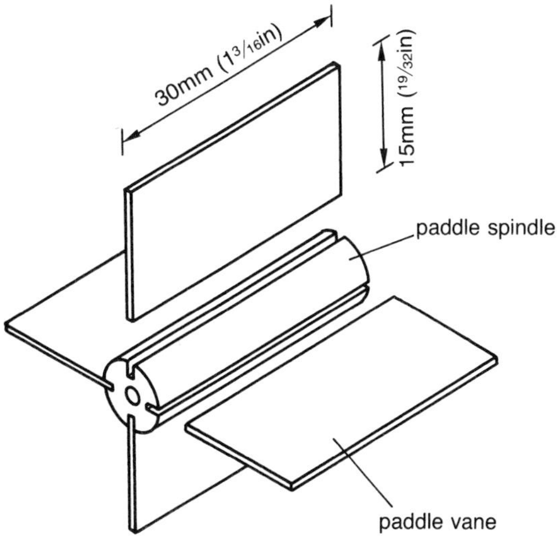

Exploded view of paddle assembly – the paddles may need to be rounded off slightly to fit within the dome.

the dowel flat on the workbench and cut four shallow grooves with the tenon saw, no more than 2mm deep.

Into these grooves fit four small rectangular vanes cut from 2mm (3/32in)-thick plywood, each measuring approximately 30×15mm (1 3/16×19/32in). Cut the vanes to size with a sharp knife, mix some wood glue and stick them into their grooves, standing the assembly on its end while the glue dries hard.

Cut two small spacers to size from 6mm (1/4in)-diameter dowelling, in which 2mm (3/32in)-diameter holes have already been drilled through the centre, to fill the gaps between the ends of the paddle and the inside wall of the domed top, so that when fully assembled, there is no freedom of movement for the axle shaft to pull out of its rear hole. Fix the paddle assembly and the two spacers on to the axle shaft with epoxy resin adhesive, sliding the shaft right through and into its rear hole. The vanes of the paddle should be aligned with the sails. Allow time for the adhesive to set.

Mark in the window and door openings where required. Cut around them with a sharp knife and gouge out the waste to a depth of 2mm (3/32in) or so.

THE FINAL STAGES

Doors and Windows

Doors and window openings can now be marked on the outer surface of the tower in various positions, and carved into the wood with chisels and gouges to a depth of 4mm (3/16in) or so. Glazing bars may be added to the windows by gluing in very thin strips of hardwood.

The Gantry

The final stage of construction is to make the gantry and the fantail wheel assembly – although you may decide not to include these. They certainly add a nice authentic touch to the windmill, but bear in mind that a very young child could easily break them off by rough handling.

The gantry, when fitted, consists of a ring cut from very thin plywood, forming the solid walkway, to which a handrail is attached with a series of tiny upright slats. Longer sloped slats below the walkway form brackets which rest on a batten that runs around the tower.

The Walkway

Mark out the ring for the walkway on a piece of 2mm (3/32in)-thick plywood, using the compasses. The inner circle has a radius of 42mm (1⅝in) and the outer circle a radius of 54mm (2⅛in), assuming that the contours of the tower conform to those of the illustrated example. As a rough guide, the gantry should be fitted approximately 70mm (2¾in) up from the bottom of the tower. As the plywood is so thin, it is advisable to cut around both lines with a sharp knife, rubbing down the edges with fine-grade sandpaper.

The Handrail

The handrail is made in the form of a hoop from material measuring 343×3×3mm (3½×⅛×⅛in), with 3mm-deep halved joints cut at each end, and the smaller batten hoop measures 292×3×3mm (1½×⅛×⅛in), similarly half-jointed. These joints, being very small, are also cut at the ends with the sharp knife. Soak the two strips thoroughly in water to make the wood pliable, and then bend them both into circular hoops, apply a little wood glue to the joints and bind them together with sticky tape while the glue dries.

The handrail is attached to the walkway with 34 slats, each measuring 10×3×3mm (13/32×⅛×⅛in) and arranged at regular intervals of 10mm (13/32in) around the outer perimeter of the walkway. Measure and mark off these intervals and cut out a square notch of 3×3mm (⅛×⅛in) at each position. Glue the 34 slats upright into the notches and fix the hooped handrail on top. Now slide the batten hoop down the tower, making sure that it is perfectly level, and glue it in place. Likewise, slide the walkway ring with the attached handrail and slats

Mark off the positions of the handrail slats on the outside edge of the plywood gantry ring, using a geometrical protractor for accuracy.

Glue the handrail slats into the notches cut around the outside edge of the gantry walkway, and then assemble the handrail ring on top with more glue.

onto the tower, gluing in position. Finally, measure the distance between the top of the batten and the underside of the walkway, where each upright slat is located, and cut 34 bracing slats, gluing these in alignment with the handrail slats.

The Fantail Assembly

The fantail assembly is a disc of 2mm (3⁄32in)-thick plywood, cut to a radius of 15mm (19⁄32in), split up into eight vanes, their edges bevelled with a sharp knife. They are mounted between two simple A-frames which are, in turn, attached at the back of the domed top with two horizontal beams, a short spacer block and two bracing struts set higher up, all the rigging being made from 3×3mm (1⁄8×1⁄8in) hardwood strip. The fantail is pivoted on a short piece of 2mm (3⁄32in)-

The assembled fantail wheel mounting frame, consisting of two A-frames with supporting beams and bracings.

diameter steel axle, which is fitted into a receiver hole at the top of each A-frame.

The windmill should now be painted. The tower could be either reddish brown, to imitate brickwork, or white; the roof, a pale silvery grey and the sails, fantail, gantry and window openings, all white.

Cutting List

Domed top: one of 72×72×42mm (2 13/16×2 13/16×1 5/8in)
Tower: one of 19×100mm (3/4×4in) diameter (1st ring)
one of 19×96mm (3/4×3 3/4in) diameter (2nd ring)
one of 19×92mm (3/4×3 5/8in) diameter (3rd ring)
one of 19×88mm (3/4×3 1/4in) diameter (4th ring)
one of 19×84mm (3/4×3 5/32in) diameter (5th ring)
one of 19×80mm (3/4×3 1/8in) diameter (6th ring)
one of 19×76mm (3/4×3in) diameter (7th ring)
one of 19×72mm (3/4×2 13/16in) diameter (8th ring)
one of 19×68mm (3/4×2 11/16in) diameter (9th ring)
one of 19×64mm (3/4×2 1/2in) diameter (10th ring)
Sail arm: two of 220×6×6mm (8 5/8×1/4×1/4in)
Sail: four of 90×25×3mm (3 9/16×1×1/8in)
Sail louvres: thirty-two of 19×5×2mm (3/4×7/32×3/32in)
Paddle vane: four of 30×15×2mm (1 3/16×19/32×3/32in)
Paddle spindle: one of 30×9mm (1 3/16×3/8in) diameter
Gantry walkway: one of 2×108mm (3/32×4 1/4in) diameter
Gantry handrail: one of 343×3×3mm (13 1/2×1/8×1/8in)
Gantry batten: on of 292×3×3mm (11 1/2×1/8×1/8in)
Gantry handrail slat: thirty-four of 10×3×3mm (13/32×1/8×1/8in)
Gantry bracing slat: thirty-four of 15×3×3mm (19/32×1/8×1/8in) approx.
Fantail wheel: one of 2×30mm (3/32×1 3/16in) diameter
Fantail mounting frame constructed from 3×3mm (1/8×1/8in) hardwood strip

Chapter Fifteen

The Horse Tricycle

What toddler could resist riding a little horse on wheels? This sturdy tricycle is designed for a child aged between about eighteen months and two years, although practical experience shows that its appeal starts much earlier and goes on a lot later!

The handlebars are made to resemble a horse's head, giving it a friendly appearance, and the seat is specially shaped to allow plenty of room for the child's legs to straddle it and even reach the ground. A curved back-rest is fitted to the rear of the seat to prevent the child from sliding off backwards, and all the edges of the wood are gently rounded for safety.

The rear wheels are mounted wide apart for stability, and the turning front axle carries a pair of wheels set one on each side of the rotating support.

The best wood to use for the tricycle is a good quality softwood that is completely free from knots, such as parana pine. This particular wood is easy to work and,

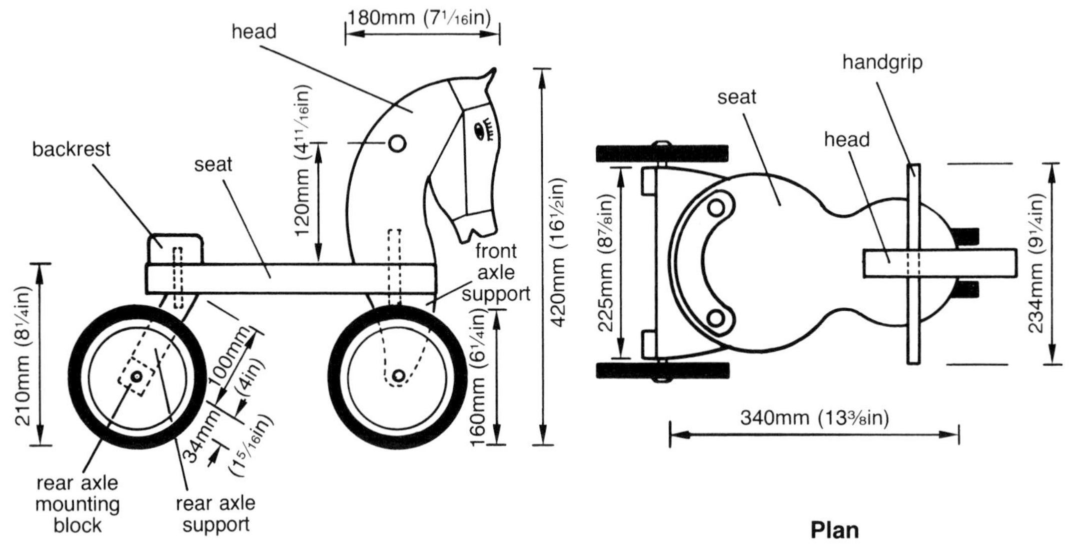

Main dimensions of the horse tricycle.

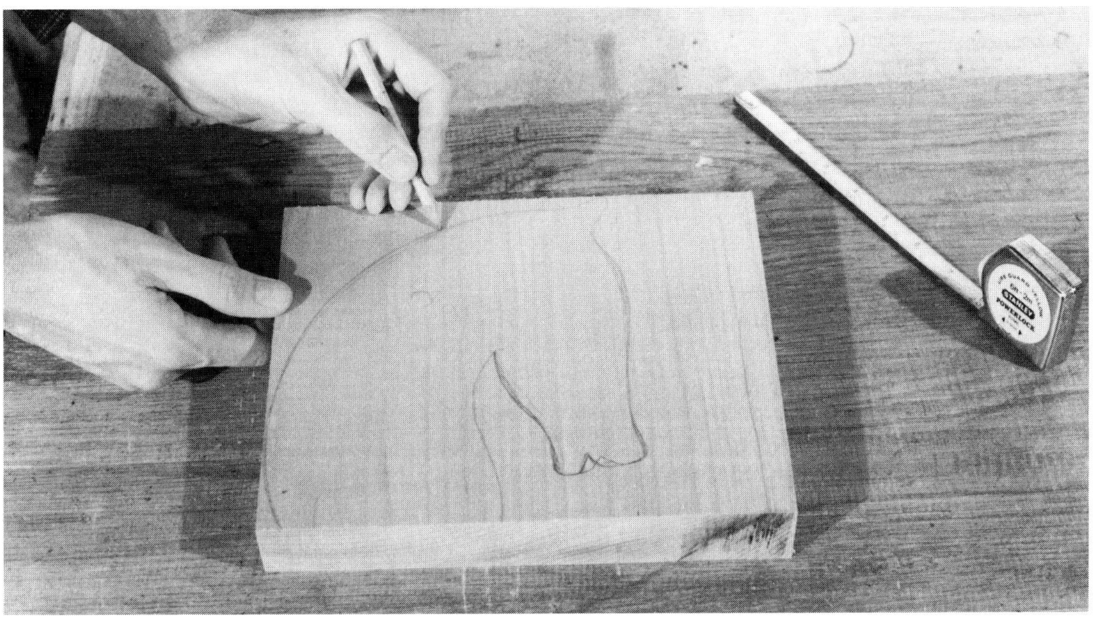

Mark the shape of the horse's head on to the wood in pencil.

coated in clear varnish, gives a warm pleasing finish; it also has sufficient strength to withstand plenty of rough use. A single piece measuring $800\times250\times34$mm ($31\frac{1}{2}\times9\frac{7}{8}\times1\frac{5}{16}$in) will be large enough to make the tricycle, provided you measure and cut economically.

CUTTING OUT

Start by cutting the piece on to which the horse's head is marked out. It is important to be accurate with the overall dimensions of the head, because this determines the way that the child will sit on the tricycle, and control it. You will find that it helps to make a paper pattern of the shape rather than draw it straight on to the wood, adjusting the appearance here and there until it looks just right.

Sketch the outline lightly on to the

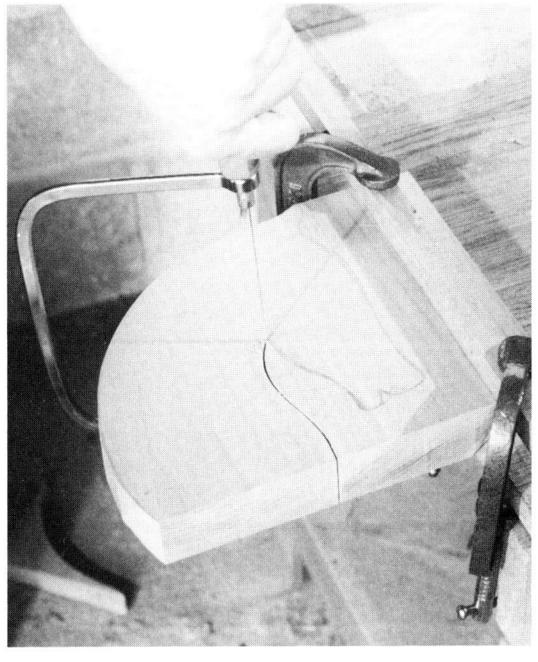

Clamp the wood to the workbench and saw around the pencilled outline.

wood in pencil, paying special attention to the curvature of the neck, the pointing forward of the ears and the opening of the mouth.

Clamp the wood firmly to the workbench and cut along the pencil lines using a coping saw or an electric jig-saw. Take extra care when sawing around the ears and mouth, and avoid cutting them too finely, otherwise there is a possibility that they will break off when the tricycle is in use.

The Seat

Next, mark out the seat. This consists of two circles of differing radii drawn in line along the direction of the grain, with their circumferences just touching. Make sure you do not confuse radius with diameter – the radius is the distance from the centre of the circle to the circumference, and the diameter is the distance across the circle, passing through the centre.

Use a pair of compasses, setting the radius to 97.5mm ($3\frac{27}{32}$in) (diameter 195mm ($7\frac{11}{16}$in)) for the rear section where the child sits, and to 72.5mm ($2\frac{27}{32}$in) (diameter 145mm ($5\frac{11}{16}$in)) for the front where the head is mounted.

Now adjust the compasses to a still smaller radius of 40mm ($1\frac{9}{16}$in), place the point in a position to the side of the circles from where an arc can be drawn to join the front circle to the rear circle. Repeat for the other side. You will end up with a pattern like the one shown in the plan illustration.

Draw the two circles that form the seat using a pair of compasses.

Cut out the whole seat in one operation, starting and finishing at the rear.

Clamp the piece to the workbench and cut carefully around the marked area with the coping saw or jig-saw, starting at the rear and working around until you reach the point where you started. If you are using a jig-saw you will need to be especially careful not to try and force it along too quickly, causing the blade to wander off the vertical, and the curved edge to acquire an unwanted slope. Cut slowly with precision and you should find that when the blade returns to the starting point, the waste comes off cleanly without a ridge. Rub down the curved edge with medium-grade sandpaper.

The Backrest

Mark out the back-rest, which is curved to match the seat with a marginally smaller radius of 94mm ($3^{11}/_{16}$in) for the outer curve and 60mm ($2^{3}/_{8}$in) for the inner, giving it a depth of 34mm ($1^{5}/_{16}$in). Set the compasses to a radius of 17mm ($^{21}/_{32}$in) and round off both ends. Cut out as before, working the saw carefully around the ends.

The Rear Axle Support

The rear axle support is mounted below the seat and projects backwards at an angle of 60 degrees for increased stability. Cut a rectangle of wood to size, ensuring

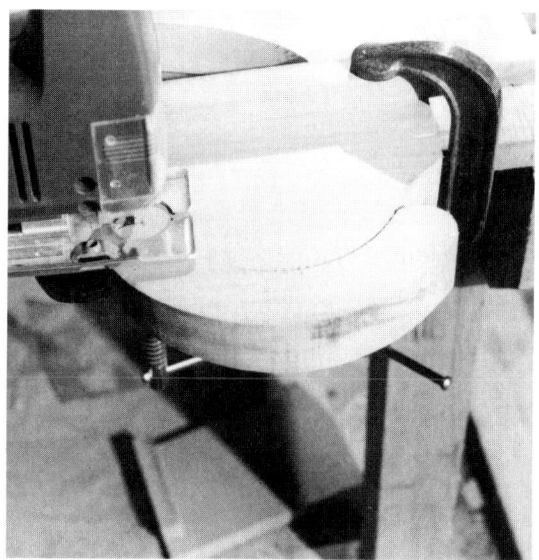

Mark and cut out the curved back-rest.

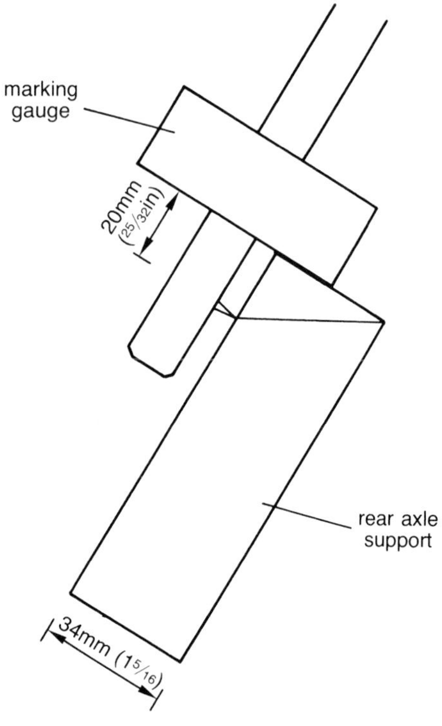

Marking the bevel on the top edge of the rear axle support.

that the top edge is planed perfectly square. Set a marking gauge to a distance of 20mm ($^{25}/_{32}$in), and run the pointer across the top of the rear surface. Clamp the piece in the workbench vice and plane off the waste, forming a 60 degree bevel along the top edge.

Cut the two blocks which fit on the lower edge of the rear axle support to carry the steel rod that serves as the axle. Finally, mark out and cut to size the front axle support, noting that the curved lines form a progression of the neck.

ASSEMBLY

The first stage of assembly is to fit the back-rest to the top of the seat, and to attach the rear axle support directly below. These three components are joined as a sandwich, using two lengths of 16mm ($^{5}/_{8}$in)-diameter dowelling, which

Mark the 60 degree bevel along the top edge of the rear axle support with the marking gauge.

Prepare the bevel along the top edge of the rear axle support using the smoothing plane.

pass right through the seat and fit into two stopped holes drilled in the underside of the back-rest, one at each end, and two holes drilled in corresponding positions at the ends of the bevelled top edge of the rear axle support.

Mark the holes very carefully. First, turn the back-rest upside down and locate the two points that coincide with the radii of curvature for the two rounded ends. As you have already marked these positions with the compasses, the points should be clearly distinguishable by tiny pin-pricks. Enlarge these into small holes by tapping a panel pin down through the surface to a depth of 4mm (3⁄16in) or so, then withdraw the pin. Cut 6mm (1⁄4in) from both pointed ends of a cocktail stick and insert these into the holes with the sharp points just protruding. Now lay the backrest in place at the rear of the seat and apply gentle downward pressure to mark the hole positions.

Remove and discard the ends of the cocktail stick. At the two points where tiny indentations have been left in the top surface of the seat, locate the tip of a 16mm (5⁄8in)-diameter centre bit and drill through the piece. Take the usual precaution and avoid boring right through in one go, but feel underneath with your finger to detect when the tip of the drill-bit is just breaking the lower surface. Turn the piece over and complete drilling from the opposite side.

Clamp the back-rest to the end of the workbench and drill two matching holes in corresponding positions to a depth of 19mm (3⁄4in). Now hold the rear axle support firmly in position on the underside of the seat, with the bevelled top edge held directly beneath the two holes. Pass a pencil through the seat holes so that it clearly marks two circles on the bevel. As you are working blind, you cannot be certain that the two pencilled circles are correctly placed on the bevel; adjust their centres with a tape measure so that they are set at a distance of 13mm (1⁄2in) from the rear edge of the bevel.

Clamp the rear axle support in the vice and drill two 16mm (5⁄8in)-diameter holes at right angles to the surface of the bevel, to a depth of 25mm (1in). You will find that the depth is somewhat restricted by the fact that you are drilling at an angle that takes you towards the front face of the piece, and you must be sure to stop drilling before breaking through the surface. If in doubt, make frequent pauses to check progress.

Cut two 75mm (3in) lengths of 16mm (5⁄8in)-diameter dowelling, place these in the holes and bring the three parts together to test the fitting of the joints. At the moment, the top corners of the rear axle support jut out beyond the edge of the seat, and these need to be trimmed back to form a neat rounded join with the bottom of the seat. Begin by pencilling in two gently sloping curves, then dismantle the joint, secure the rear axle support in the vice and pare off the waste bit by bit with a sharp chisel, switching to sandpaper to create smooth, flowing curves that match exactly the curvature of the seat. At the same time, rub down the back-rest thoroughly to round off both top edges.

The axles for the wheels are cut from

Place the rear axle support securely in the vice and pare off the waste from the two top corners with a sharp chisel to produce smooth curves.

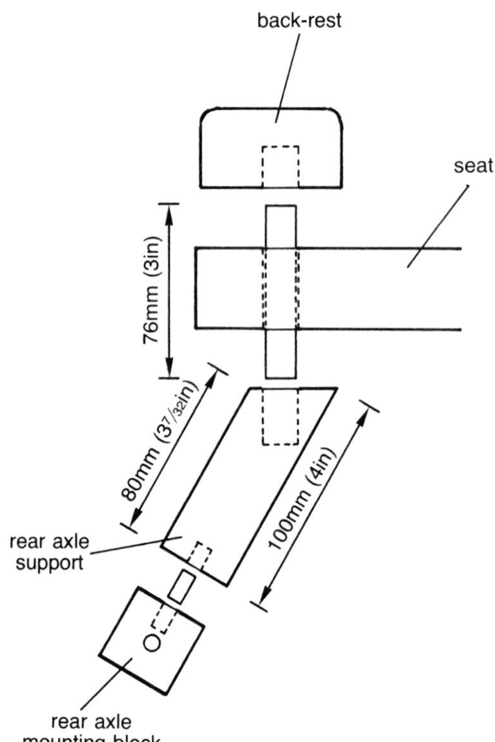

Exploded view of seat, back-rest and rear axle support with one axle block.

lengths of 9mm (3⁄8in)-diameter steel rod, and holes for these are drilled through the middle of the two rear axle mounting blocks, and similarly through the bottom of the front axle support. Starting with the rear axle mounting blocks, mark the centre of two opposite faces on each block, and drill halfway down into each face with a 9mm (3⁄8in)-diameter auger bit until the two holes meet up.

Slide the two drilled blocks on to a length of steel axle rod, about 310–320mm (12³⁄16–12⁵⁄8in) in length, to check that they fit, and space them 225mm (8⁷⁄8in) apart from each other to match the width of the rear axle support.

Join the two blocks to the lower edge of the rear axle support, one at each end, using dowel joints. For rigidity, use two 6mm (¼in)-diameter dowels, each 19mm

Attach each mounting block to the lower edge of the rear axle support using two 6mm (¼in) diameter dowels.

(¾in) long, per joint. Drill each hole to a depth of 10mm (13/32in) and assemble using strong wood glue. Keep the rear axle in place while the glue dries.

Measure and mark the position of the axle hole in the front axle support. This is located 96mm (3¾in) down from the top edge. Drill out the hole with the 9mm (⅜in)-diameter auger bit, keeping the handbrace absolutely perpendicular to the face of the wood and stopping just as the bit breaks the surface on the opposite side. Turn over to complete the drilling.

The head is joined to the front axle support with a length of 16mm (⅝in)-diameter dowelling that passes through the seat to form a pivot. Mark the point at the centre of the lower edge of the head, then hold the piece firmly upside down in the vice and bore out a 16mm (⅝in)-diameter hole to a depth of 38mm (1½in). Mark corresponding hole posi-

Clamp the head upside-down in the vice, then mark in the position of the dowel pivot and drill carefully into the end-grain with the 16mm (⅝in) diameter centre bit.

Bore out the 16mm (5/8in) diameter pivot hole in the front of the seat.

tions in the upper edge of the front axle support, noting that there should be a continuation of the curved lines and on the seat. Drill a hole to a matching depth of 38mm (1½in) in the front axle support and right through the seat.

Cut a 112mm (4⅜in) length of 16mm (⅝in)-diameter dowelling and use it to fit the head to the front axle support, leaving a gap of 36mm (1 7/16in) in between. This gap is slightly greater than the thickness of the seat. Place the head and the axle support flat on the workbench and, using a 6mm (¼in)-diameter auger bit, drill through the side of the dowel joint, including the dowel, 13mm (½in) from the lower edge of the head and 13mm (½in) from the upper edge of the front axle support. This will allow small dowel pegs to be inserted during final assembly, to hold the main pivoting dowel rigidly in the joint, so that it can withstand the constant turning to and fro of the head and front wheels.

Measure and mark the position of the handgrip, which is located 120mm (4¾in) up from the lower edge of the head. Drill through at the marked position with the 16mm (⅝in)-diameter centre bit to make a hole to take a length of dowelling. The handgrip need only project 100mm (4in) on each side of the head, giving a total required length of 234mm (9 3/16in).

Up to this point, the rear axle support and back-rest have not been assembled

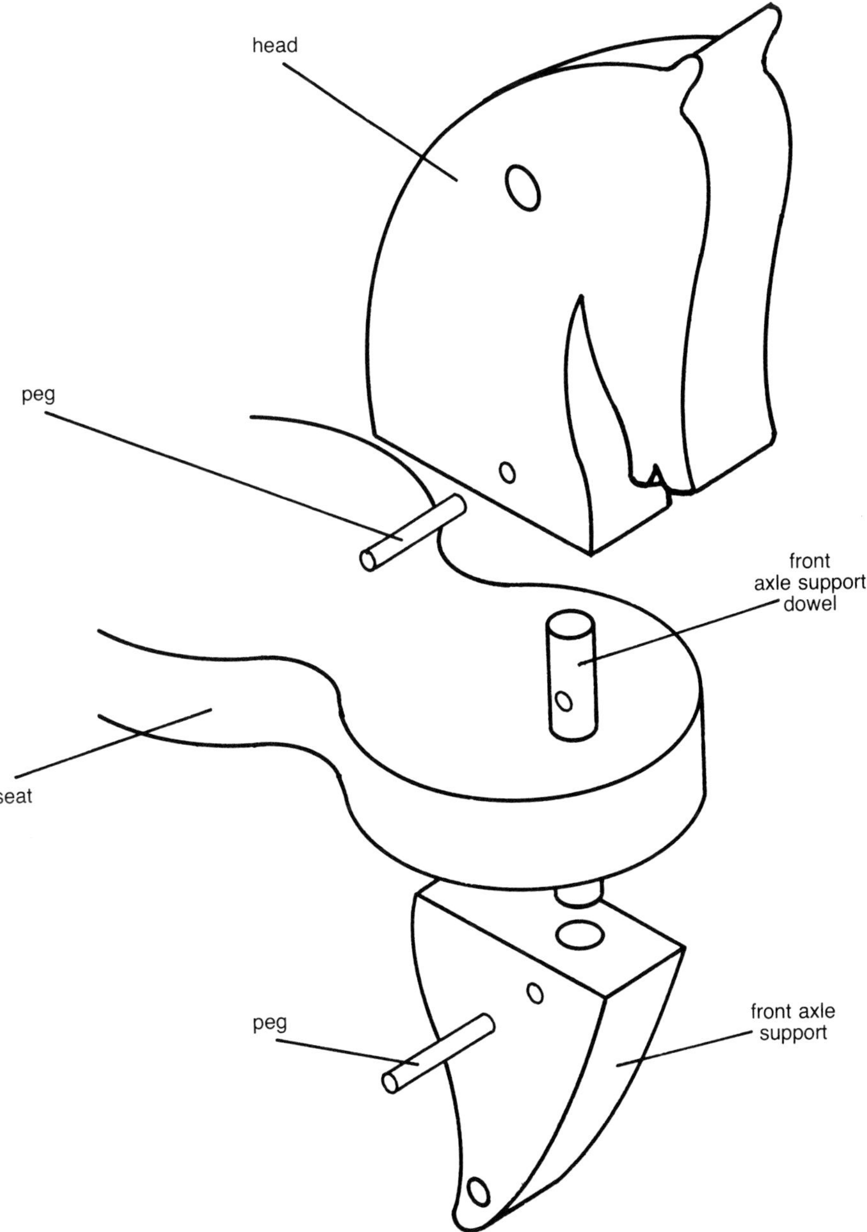

Exploded view of head and front axle support being assembled to the seat.

With the head and front axle support joined by the prepared length of pivot dowelling, and both parts lying flat on the workbench, drill the 6mm (¼in) diameter peg holes.

Assemble the back-rest and rear axle support to the seat, using the two prepared dowels.

Paint the horse's features and bridle on to the head, using black enamel paint.

to the seat, although the rear axle mounting blocks have been joined to the bottom edge of the support. Mix a small quantity of powdered resin wood glue and apply it to the underside of the backrest, the bevelled edge of the rear axle support and to the two lengths of dowel that help to locate all three pieces in their correct positions. Set the assembly to one side while the glue dries and hardens thoroughly.

Before assembling the head, sand the surface with fine-grade paper until it is completely smooth, and draw the face on both sides in pencil, marking in an eye with eyelashes, the bridle and the mane. Experiment first on a piece of paper to be sure of getting the right expression. When you are satisfied that both sides are identical and that the horse has a suitably friendly appearance, carefully paint in the features using black enamel paint applied with a very fine brush. Use the tip of a cocktail stick for the thinnest lines.

When the paint is completely dry, mix some more wood glue and assemble the 234mm (9³⁄₁₆in) piece of 16mm (⅝in)-diameter dowelling into the handgrip hole, measuring to make sure that an exact 100mm (4in) projects on either side. Wipe off any surplus glue to avoid staining the wood.

Next, glue the 16mm (⅝in)-diameter dowel pivot to the head, pegging it with a 36mm (1⁷⁄₁₆in) length of 6mm (¼in)-

Use washers between the moving parts on the pivot joint, to resist friction.

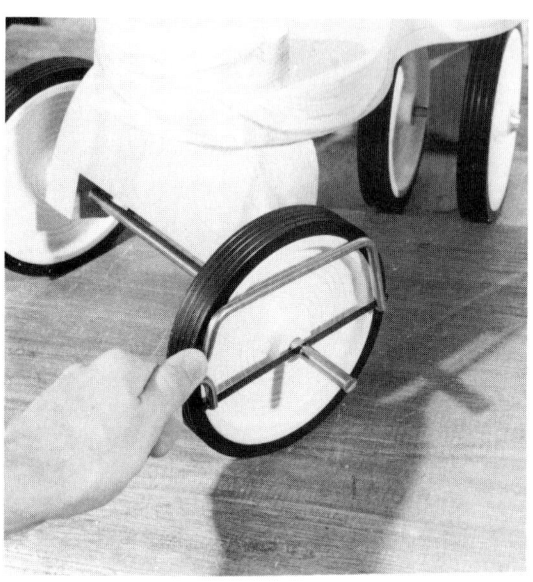

Saw the steel axle rod to length with a hacksaw before fitting the hub caps.

diameter dowelling glued and tapped right through the thickness of the head. Place a very thin nylon or fibre washer between the head and the top of the seat and mount the head. Repeat with a second matching washer beneath the seat and finally glue the front axle support to the dowel pivot, securing with a second 6mm (¼in)-diameter peg.

Once the glue is thoroughly dry and hardened, cut the pegs flush with the sides of the head and the axle support, and sandpaper the surfaces of the tricycle, except for the head, to prepare for varnishing. Use at least three coats of clear matt varnish and sand down lightly with very fine paper between coats for a perfect finish.

The Wheels

Attach four 160mm (6¼in)-diameter rubber-tyred wheels to the axles and measure an extra 9mm (⅜in) for the spring hub caps. Remove the wheels and cut off the excess lengths of axle with a hacksaw, filing the ends flat. Put the wheels back on and tap the spring hub caps on to the ends of the axle with a small wooden mallet, making sure that they are free to turn easily.

The horse tricycle is ready for its rider.

Cutting List

Seat: one of 340×195×34mm (13⅜×7¹¹⁄₁₆×1⁵⁄₁₆in)
Head: one of 210×180×34mm (8¼×7¹⁄₁₆×1⁵⁄₁₆in)
Back-rest: one of 160×68×34mm (6⁵⁄₁₆×2¹³⁄₁₆×1⁵⁄₁₆in)
Front axle support: one of 110×85×34mm (4⁵⁄₁₆×3⁵⁄₁₆×1⁵⁄₁₆in)
Rear axle support: one of 100×225×34mm (4×8⅞×1⁵⁄₁₆in)
Rear axle mounting block: two of 34×34×34mm (1⁵⁄₁₆×1⁵⁄₁₆×1⁵⁄₁₆in)
Handgrip: one of 234×16mm (9¼×⅝in) diameter
Front axle support joint: one 112×16mm (4⅜×⅝in) diameter
Rear axle support joint: two of 76×16mm (3×⅝in) diameter

Glossary

Adhesive A substance used for sticking two or more pieces of wood together, made from synthetic constituents.
Auger bit A boring tool which fits into a drill and is shaped in the form of a long spiral with a cutting tip.

Bench hook A flat wooden workbench accessory, consisting of a small wooden board with a narrow block fitted at each end, on alternate sides, used for holding pieces of wood steady for cutting.
Bench stop A small metal flap or a wooden block set in a hole cut in the surface of the workbench, designed to act as a stop for long pieces of wood, thus preventing slippage across the top of the bench during planing operations.
Bevel A slope that is worked between an edge and a side, or an end-grain and a side of a piece of wood, usually with a plane or chisel, affecting the entire thickness.
Bradawl A small marking tool consisting of a short handle fitted with a spike, used for making pilot holes before commencing drilling.
Butt joint A joint formed when the squared and planed edges or sides of two pieces of wood are brought together, or the edge of one piece and the side of the other.

Chamfer A bevel that is worked across only a portion of the edge's thickness, rather than all of it.
Chisel A handtool with a razor-sharp blade tip, used for chopping out or paring away waste wood.
Chuck The part of a drill or lathe which holds the bit or the work.
Circumference The distance around a complete circle.
Contact adhesive A type of adhesive that is applied to both joining surfaces and allowed to dry before the surfaces are brought into contact. Firm pressure makes for an immediate bond.
Countersunk The term used to describe a bevelled edge given to a hole to receive the head of a similarly shaped screw, so that it can be recessed below the surface of the wood.
Cramp A clamping device incorporating a movable part which may be screwed one way or the other to tighten or loosen, thus enabling a joint to be held securely together during assembly.

Diameter The distance across a circle, passing through its centre.
Dowel hole The hole that is drilled in a piece of wood to receive a dowel peg.
Dowel joint A joint in which the constituent parts are precisely located and fastened by one or more lengths of dowelling.

Dowelling A pin, usually made from hardwood, used to fasten together two pieces of wood by fitting into a hole drilled in each one.

Edge The surface of a piece of wood which is identified as its thickness.
Edge moulding A decorative profile given to the edge of the wood by working a special tool along it, such as the router or plough plane, fitted with an appropriate cutter.
End-grain When a piece of wood is sawn perpendicularly to its length, the cut is made across the direction of the wood grain, and the exposed surface, which displays the annual growth rings, is termed the end-grain.

Fence The part of a tool that bears against the workpiece, thus maintaining a set distance for marking out or cutting.
Flush A state in which two surfaces are level with one another.
Fluting A groove worked along the length of the wood grain, usually for decorative purposes.

G-clamp A small metal clamp, shaped in the form of a letter G, which has a screw-thread for tightening. It is often employed for the holding together of two or more pieces of wood, especially to fasten them down on the workbench.
Glue A substance which is, strictly speaking, derived from organic matter, used for sticking together pieces of wood.
Grain The arrangement of fibres running along the length of a piece of wood, often determining its characteristic appearance.
Groove A channel cut in the wood, either in the making of a joint, or to decorate the surface.

Hacksaw A handtool in which the cutting blade is held in a metal frame which has a handgrip at one end. The blade is removable, and has fine teeth.
Halved joint The halved joint is used to join together two lengths of wood, usually at right-angles, by removing half the thickness from both pieces so that when they are assembled, their surfaces are flush.
Hardboard A material made from compressed wood fibres, normally smooth on one side and textured on the other.
Hardwood Timber that is derived from deciduous trees, which shed their leaves once a year. The term does not relate particularly to the degree of hardness, although many hardwoods come from trees which are relatively slow-growing, and produce rather dense, close-grained wood.
Headstock The part of a lathe which, driven by the motor, is responsible for holding the work and applying the turning effect.
Housing joint A housing joint is formed by fitting the end of one piece of wood into a groove cut along the length, or across the grain, of the second piece.

Imperial measurement The standard of measurement based on the inch.

Joint A joining together of two or more pieces of wood to create a structure. There are many common varieties of joint.

Kerf A groove, or channel, made by a saw blade cutting through the wood, its width being determined by the set of the blade's teeth.
Knot The point at which a branch joined the trunk of a tree, leaving a dense

area of matter normally considered as an undesirable feature of the material.

Lap joint A joint formed between pieces of wood in which one edge or side overlaps another.
Lathe A machine designed for turning and shaping wood or metal.

Mallet A hammer made entirely from wood, usually with a large head and a strong, stout handle. The mallet is used to strike the chisel, and to apply the necessary force when assembling joints.
Metric measurement The standard of measurement based on the metre.
Mitre joint A mitre joint is formed by two pieces of wood having their ends cut at an angle of 45 degrees so that they meet to form a right-angled corner. The degree of angle may actually be varied to suit different purposes.
Mortise-and-tenon joint This consists of a mortise, or opening, cut into one piece of wood, and a tenon, or tongue, equal in size to the mortise, cut in the second piece.

Nail A metal pin, pointed at one end, available in various lengths and gauges and different types of head, which is used for fastening wood.

Panel pin A thin, small-headed nail used for attaching sheet material such as plywood on to a framework of wood.
Pilot hole A marker hole, of shallow depth, intended simply to fix the position of the proper hole and serve as a guide into which the drill-bit can be placed.
Plywood This is a timber product composed of thin wood veneers arranged in such a way that the grain runs in alternate directions, each layer at right-angles to the next, and bonded together under great pressure. Plywood always has an odd number of veneers.
Protractor A measuring instrument used for determining and marking angles.

Radius The straight-line distance from the centre of a circle to any point on its circumference.
Rebate A groove cut along an edge.

Sandpaper An abrasive sheet made by coating a special paper with a hard grit of varying coarseness, depending on the degree of abrasion required.
Scotch glue A glue derived from animal matter, and supplied as a solid block which must be broken up and soaked thoroughly in water before applying heat to dissolve it into a usable substance.
Scrap wood Any piece of off-cut wood which is employed to protect the workpiece from suffering surface damage from clamps, the jaws of the vice, or blows from a mallet during assembly, or indeed any other similar infliction. The 'scrap' should always be clean and smooth.
Screw A long metal wood-fastening device which has a spiral thread cut along part of its length, and a head of various types, with either a single or a crossed slot cut in it to receive the screwdriver.
Screw-eye A metal ring in which one end projects and terminates in a screw-thread.
Side The surface of a piece of wood which is identified as its width.
Softwood Timber derived from evergreen trees, which tend to be relatively fast-growing, giving light, loosely grained wood.

Spur The sharp, pointed part of a marking tool.
Square A marking tool, consisting of a rectangular wooden handle, edged in brass, which has a steel blade attached to it at right-angles, with two parallel edges.

Tailstock The part of a lathe at the opposite end to the headstock, which also holds the work in position, and may be moved to and fro to engage the work or release it.
Tape measure A measuring instrument made from metal (the wooden version is usually known as a ruler), marked in metric or imperial gradations.
Template A solid outline cut from thick card or thin plywood to enable a complex shape to be marked on to the workpiece, perhaps many times.
Tenon saw A medium-sized saw, equipped with fine teeth and a reinforced back to give rigidity and thus ensure the straight, accurate cut required in the preparation of joints.
Tongue A narrow projection of wood.
Tongued-and-grooved joint A joint that is formed when the edge of one piece of wood has a groove cut centrally along its length to receive a corresponding tongue cut along the joining edge of the second piece.
Trammel A marking template for describing an ellipse, with three fixed positions set along a straight edge.

Veneer A thin sheet of wood laid on top of an inferior quality board to provide a high-quality surface.
Veneer pin A very small version of the panel pin.
Vice A tool that is fixed to the workbench to hold pieces of wood firmly in position as they are being worked on.

Warping The process that results in wood that is twisted or bent out of shape. The problem is usually caused by exposure to dampness on one surface.
Waste Unwanted wood removed in the process of cutting out a joint, or trimming a piece of wood to size.
Wood finish Treatment, such as varnish, paint or polish, given to the exposed surface of the wood.
Wood-turning The process of shaping a piece of wood by spinning it on the lathe, and presenting one of a number of woodturning tools to its fast-rotating surface to cut it down to the required shape and size.
Workbench A sturdy wooden bench, or table, fitted with useful accessories such as a woodworking vice, upon which woodwork is carried out.

INDEX